RURAL ENERGY SERVICES

Rural Energy Services

*A handbook for sustainable
energy development*

TERESA ANDERSON, ALISON DOIG,
DAI REES and SMAIL KHENNAS

IT PUBLICATIONS 1999

Intermediate Technology Publications Ltd
103/105 Southampton Row, London WC1B 4HH, UK

© The British Council and the Intermediate Technology Development Group 1999

A CIP record for this book is available from the British Library

ISBN 1 85339 462 9

Typeset and illustrated by Dorwyn Ltd, Rowlands Castle, Hants, UK
Printed by SRP, Exeter

Contents

ACKNOWLEDGEMENTS vii

INTRODUCTION: RURAL ENERGY OPTIONS ix

PART I   DELIVERY OPTIONS 1

1 Market and needs evaluation 3
   Energy service requirements 3
   Energy service survey guide 8
   Participatory and co-operative planning and management of
      rural electricity supplies 11

2 Financing energy supplies for rural communities 18
   Financing options 18
   Financial performance 22
   Policy and market instruments 27
   Private versus public sector 36

3 Assessing impact and success 40
   Environmental impacts 40
   Factors affecting scheme success 45

PART II   TECHNICAL OPTIONS 51

4 Conventional technologies 53
   Diesel 53
   Kerosene and liquid petroleum gas 58
   Grid connection 63

5 Renewable energy sources 67
   Biomass 67
   Biogas and liquid biofuels 75
   Wind pumping 81
   Wind power for electricity generation 87
   Micro-hydro power 90
   Solar photovoltaic energy 95
   Solar thermal energy 105

6 Key technology issues 110
   Grid versus stand-alone electrical generation and supply 110
   Cost comparison of energy options 116

PART III CASE STUDIES

		123
1	Chalan micro-hydro scheme (Peru)	125
2	Arun III (Nepal)	128
3	Rural stoves (Kenya)	134
4	Photovoltaics (Indonesia and Zimbabwe)	142
5	Electric cooking with micro-hydro power (Nepal)	146

Appendix   Group exercise: PV lantern design and marketing   151

REFERENCES AND RESOURCES   157

Acknowledgements

The authors wish to thank all those whose advice and material has contributed to this work; and have tried to acknowledge traceable sources as clearly as possible.

This book originated as a set of factsheets used at a series of workshops in India and Uganda, as resource material, and through ideas and experience gained at these workshops evolved into a Handbook.

The authors wish to thank in particular the Department for International Development (DFID), in the UK and the British Council for financing the workshops and this publication.

The assistance of DFID India, Centre for Energy and Environmental Science and Technology (CEESAT), Tiruchirappalli, Maulana Azad College of Technology (MACT), Bhopal and IT Kenya in organising the workshops, is appreciated. Thanks are also due to Vinoj Manning (IDE), Lalith Guneratne, Shyam Sunder, (CEDAR), Ray Holland, Daniel Start, and Rona Wilkinson (ITC) for their inputs and ideas.

Introduction

Rural energy options

In most countries of the world, people living in urban areas generally have access to efficient and modern energy supplies. Rural populations, however, are generally less fortunate and, especially in less-industrialized countries, rely on 'traditional' fuels, or energy and electricity production systems that are costly and inefficient.

In Africa, for instance, it has been estimated that only around 10 per cent of urban households have an electricity supply, and that the proportion of rural households supplied is far less. A survey carried out by the International Centre for Research on the Environment and Development produced the data in Table 0.1.

Table 0.1: Proportion of rural population with access to electricity supply in regions of the world

Region	Percentage of rural population with access to electricity
Latin America	27
Asia	19
North Africa	21
Rest of Africa	4

In addition, it must be noted that where supply systems do reach rural areas (as in Zimbabwe), households are often unable to afford the cost of connection. In Zimbabwe, 90 per cent of urban households use electricity, but only around 6 per cent of rural households have a connection. It follows, therefore, that rural populations, which represent around 50 per cent of the world's population, usually do not meet their energy needs with electricity.

This book examines the ways in which rural energy needs can be met, and the issues surrounding the process.

The book forms part of an overall approach to learning about energy options that includes workshop sessions, lecture sessions, factsheets, and working through case studies and examples. It can be read in isolation from the training initiative, however, and used to follow up on training sessions.

The structure of the book

The book is divided into three main parts:

Part I. Delivery Options
Part II. Technical Options
Part III. Case Studies

The text is organized so that information on delivery issues is separated from that on technical issues (the 'software' and the 'hardware'). It is important to emphasize that the success of rural energy supply systems depends on both of these sets of issues, however, and that careful attention should be given to all aspects examined here. The delivery options are examined before the technical options, as these are often the key to the success or failure of energy provision schemes.

There are many books available on energy technologies. Renewable and de-centralized energy options are becoming more accessible and are now routinely used in developing countries. Technical know-how alone, however, will not result in sustainable energy supplies for rural communities.

For an energy supply scheme to be sustainable, it must be planned and managed so that it not only meets energy needs, but also pays for itself and for its replacement; that it does not have adverse environmental impacts; and that it allows energy consumers to expand their energy use when they need to do so in order to support income generation activities.

In short, the planning and management of an energy supply scheme can have as great an impact on the likelihood of its success as can the choice of technology and level of competence of its installation, commissioning, operation and maintenance.

Part I – Delivery Options

This section presents some of the approaches to rural energy supply that are in current use or under development.

'Market and needs evaluation', the first chapter, outlines the ways in which current thinking on rural energy provision focuses on a 'needs-driven' approach, rather than pushing a certain type of technological solution. In order to do this, the energy needs of rural communities must first be analysed. In the section titled *Energy service requirements* we examine the energy needs that may typically be found in rural communities, and the ways in which they can be identified and prioritized in the light of other needs that exist in the community. We also discuss the ways in which an integrated approach may be taken to planning energy service provision, and ways in which the most appropriate energy options may be used to meet energy needs, given the resource base available to the community. We provide a framework for a typical energy survey in *Energy service survey guide*. This lists issues that should be addressed by a good energy survey, and provides a guide to the minimum outputs that can be expected from a survey.

The section on *Participatory and co-operative planning and management of rural electricity supplies* explores the issues that surround community planning, ownership, and management of electricity supplies. Electricity represents by far the most complex way of meeting energy service needs, but it is increasingly in demand in rural areas. The techniques used to carry out community planning and management of electricity supplies can therefore be extended to their simpler counterparts (e.g. biomass resource management or wind pumping systems). This section is based on work currently under way in several countries, and which is now being extended to urban areas.

Chapter 2, 'Financing energy supplies for rural communities', discusses the issues surrounding energy system financing. The debate on whether rural electrification constitutes a development of national infrastructure (and thus merits subsidy) or whether it should be left to market forces is far from over, and we present some of the issues underlying this debate in this section. *Financing options* outlines some of the basic concepts and vocabulary used in the debate, and *Financial performance* describes ways in which the scheme's financial viability (essential to its long-term sustainability) can be assessed. *Policy and market instruments* examines the ways in which governments can set up 'enabling environments' in which the market can operate to meet the needs of even the poorest sections of society. The section *Private versus public sector* sets out some of the issues that surround the provision of energy either as a public service or via the free market, and the pros and cons of both approaches.

Chapter 3, 'Assessing impact and success', contains two sections. *Environmental impacts* examines the impacts that even renewable energy sources can have on local, national, and global environments. *Factors affecting scheme success* deals with just how a scheme can be classed as a success or otherwise.

Part II – Technical Options

This part provides an overview of the technical options that are available to meet rural energy service needs, and is also in three chapters.

Chapter 4, 'Conventional technologies', deals with technologies that are appropriate to small-scale decentralized energy service provision but which are not classed as 'renewable'. Although renewable resources are hailed as the answer to many rural energy service needs, in fact they are often costly and sometimes do not provide the level of reliability that may be required by the community. The section on *Diesel* describes the fuel that is most commonly used to meet mechanical power requirements in rural areas. *Kerosene and liquid petroleum gas* describes fuels that are used predominantly for lighting – although it also covers some use of the fuels to meet the need for cooking heat. *Grid connection*, an option that is frequently ignored when considering the energy needs of rural communities, is examined in the light of low-cost options, and options such as co-operative management or local 'mini-grids' are described.

The chapter on 'Renewable energy sources' examines technologies commonly used to harness renewable resources to meet rural energy needs. It begins with the most commonly used renewable resource, *Biomass*, and then treats a more focused use of this in the section on *Biogas and liquid biofuels*. Both of these resources are in widespread use in rural areas, although the knowledge required to produce and use them efficiently is always developing. The two sections that deal with wind power, *Wind pumping* and *Wind power for electricity generation*, describe the ways in which the wind can be harnessed, as it has been for centuries, to lift water to supply people, animals, and crops, and how the wind can be harnessed to produce electricity. The *Micro-hydro power* section combines a description of how water power can be used to produce mechanical and electrical power, and focuses almost exclusively on smaller installations that are categorized as 'mini' and 'micro' hydro sites.

The section on *Solar photovoltaic energy* explains the way in which photovoltaic (PV) technology is used to produce electricity. While this technology is still quite expensive, it has been decreasing in cost for some time, and is the focus of many large-scale funding initiatives worldwide. The section *Solar thermal energy* describes how the sun's energy can be channelled to produce useful heat, and gives a short summary of applications such as water and space heating, solar cooking and cooling, and solar crop drying.

The part dealing with technology options ends with a short chapter about 'Key technology issues' that influence the type of energy technology that can be used to meet energy service requirements. The section on *Grid versus stand-alone electrical generation and supply* discusses the relative merits of centralized and decentralized electricity supplies. The *Cost comparison of energy options* section sets out typical costs for each of the energy technologies and how this can be assessed relative to the technology lifetime.

Part III – Case Studies

The book is rounded off by a set of case studies that illustrate some of the issues surrounding the provision of energy services in rural areas. The case of the *Chalan micro-hydro scheme* describes a village hydroelectricity supply in Peru. *Arun III* examines the issue of 'appropriate scale' of energy developments by way of a large-scale hydroelectric scheme in Nepal. The case study on *Rural stoves* looks at the use of wood-burning stoves in Western Kenya, and the way in which the manufacture of improved cooking stoves can generate income for women stove producers. The *Photovoltaics* case study describes the use of PV to meet domestic and institutional power needs in Indonesia and Zimbabwe, and *Electric cooking with micro-hydro power* describes the use of low-power cooking to achieve improved load management in a decentralized village power scheme in Nepal.

The Appendix contains material for a *Group exercise* which may help to illustrate many of the issues examined in the book.

PART I

DELIVERY OPTIONS

1

Market and needs evaluation

Energy service requirements

Energy planning is often viewed as simply the provision and installation of energy technologies, expressed as the:

- percentage of communities electrified
- number of solar cookers distributed
- number of small hydro power units installed,
- number of tonnes of dung supplied to biogasifiers, etc.

The focus is on the technology, with the effective end uses of the energy considered as an afterthought. What is not considered is which *services* are actually required from the various energy technologies. Too many energy projects have failed because an energy technology was supplied to an area without an assessment of actual energy requirements having been made, so that the technology is seen to fail because:

- People have little or no need for the particular energy source.
- People have no means to develop beneficial or income-generating uses for the power.
- The energy supplied by the technology is insufficient.
- The energy is available at the wrong time of the day, or year, to be of use.
- People do not possess the relevant skills to maintain and operate the installation.

An example is the micro-hydro power system that is overloaded for lighting in the evenings, but lies unused during the day because no other end use was planned for the power. Another is the solar cooker which has to be used outside in the heat of the sun during the middle of the day, using cooking techniques very different to the local practice.

In such cases the technologies do not supply the energy services that the villages actually require. This approach often means that the technology is not economically viable, as it is underutilized, or it is so unreliable that the villagers stop using the technology and return to their traditional energy sources. In order to fulfil actual energy needs successfully, the approach to provision of energy options for rural communities must emphasize the supply of energy services.

What is an energy service?

Villagers do not need micro-hydro, they need milled flour. They do not need a photovoltaic cell, they need lighting in the house. They do not need a biogasifier, they need to cook.

3

An energy service is the function for which energy is required. It is the need that the villagers have for energy. Examples of energy services include: lighting, cooking, space heating, mechanical power, television or radio operation, and pumped water. To compare energy options there has to be a consideration not only of the reliability of the technology option, but also of the ability of the energy technology to provide sufficient energy in the right place and at the right time to achieve the required quality of output.

For example, the energy service required may be:

○ a kilogramme of flour ground to a particular fines
○ light of sufficient brightness to read by, supplied between the hours of 7 p.m. and 11 p.m.
○ provision of an exact temperature-reliable refrigerator system for medicines, or
○ the cooking of a family meal, without significantly changing local cooking times or practices.

The targets for energy planning are therefore not structured in terms of kilowatt hours supplied, or numbers of houses with the technology installed, but in terms of the service provided.

Assessing energy service requirements

The energy needs of rural people are directly linked to their social and economic lives; they will vary greatly between different social groups and between different locations. Energy demand is subject to changes in the user's socio-economic status and it is also influenced by overall technical and economic developments, such as the introduction of new or improved appliances designed to be more energy efficient or environmentally friendly. In order to determine energy service needs, it is necessary to take a closer look at how the energy is to be used and in what technical and socio-economic conditions it is required. This is a continuous process, because site-specific conditions change with time.

It is important not to confuse potential demand with present consumption. Consumption at any time may be affected by prevailing prices and the availability of fuels and technologies. Users may want or need more energy than they can afford to pay for (there is a big difference between a need and an effective demand).

It is worth noting that there will be a maximum amount that rural communities are either willing or able to pay for energy services. If this amount is less than the amount required to cover the capital and running costs of a new energy technology, then the energy project will not be commercially sustainable. In such cases, either a less expensive solution must be found to supply energy needs, or the project must be subsidized. Subsidies are usually applied only to projects that offer specific social or environmental benefits to the community.

Understanding such users' needs can be achieved only by proper surveys of consumption, demand, and needs. Rural energy demand can be broken down into several sectors, including household, subsistence farming, agriculture, livestock, industry, commerce, offices, transport, services such as schools and

4

Energy survey taking place in a village

hospitals, and so on. Each category has its own set of requirements and constraints. Assessing rural energy service requirements is where participative approaches to energy planning are essential to match service needs with the appropriate energy supply system.

An energy survey will determine what demand there is for new energy sources. It will answer such questions as: how much energy is needed, where it is needed, what form is needed (mechanical, heat, cooling, electrical, etc.), and whether there is a genuine ability and willingness to pay for the proposed new energy supply. It will also investigate methods by which the new energy supply could bring benefits to the less advantaged people in the village, and it should expose disadvantages of the new system (such as loss of jobs).

The energy survey should not be a formal questionnaire, but a checklist which can be used for more informal information collection. In this way the survey will find out about the villagers' interests, in their own terms, while still covering all the areas of interest to the energy planners. Care must be taken to account for the marginalized groups in the community, including women and lower social groups. A guidance checklist can be found in the next section.

Successful assessment of energy service needs is illustrated by an experience in Pura village near Bangalore, south India. Initial attempts to promote community biogas systems failed. The gas was originally promoted as a substitute for fuel wood for cooking, but the village had a relatively abundant source of wood. Subsequent discussions with the villagers discovered that the main concern was the lack of clean, reliable, and accessible water supplies. The biogas was then used to fuel a diesel generator, to supply electricity to households and to power a tubewell pump. All households participating in the scheme received a tap with clean water in front of their house.

Integrating energy planning into other development sectors

Energy planning cannot be divorced from other aspects of rural development, such as agriculture, rural small industry, and services including health clinics and schools.

For example, a health clinic may require energy services for:

○ medical refrigeration
○ sterilization
○ heating water, and
○ lighting.

These needs may be satisfied by a number of energy sources, including diesel generators, grid electrification, photovoltaic arrays, hydro- or wind electric generators, and solar water heaters.

Where energy services are required by the various sector development initiatives, there is an opportunity to develop rural energy supply options to supply both existing needs as well as those to be developed in the initiative. In this way, the benefits of the energy supply can be maximized, with the overall benefits from the scheme extended to supply more than just basic energy needs. In many development projects, energy is not simply an add-on, but an essential ingredient

for success. In such cases, the energy dimension of a rural development programme should be integrated into projects from an early stage.

Matching energy options to energy services

The best choice among the available options will depend on a number of factors,
most of which are covered in other chapters.

These will include the:

○ availability of sufficient energy at times when the energy service is required
○ comparative capital and running costs of each option
○ local availability of the technology and maintenance support, and
○ quality of energy service provided.

Again, a participative approach to choosing energy options for a community may
be most effective for selecting the most appropriate energy supply system acceptable to the village.

An example of an innovative approach to matching energy options to energy
needs is the development of low wattage cookers for use in households connected to micro-hydro power schemes in Nepal. The main energy need in houses
in rural Nepal is for cooking, which accounts for two-thirds of the energy demand. Electric cooking has the potential to reduce the pressure on increasingly

The bijuli dekchi *is an innovative solution to the problem of the scarcity of
fuel wood in Nepal*

Photograph: Intermediate Technology/Caroline Penn

7

scarce fuelwood supplies. Unfortunately, the micro-hydro power plants do not produce enough power to supply each household with a standard 1kW electric cooking ring. To get round this problem, and to match energy need with appropriate energy supply – in this case micro-hydro power – a low wattage cooker was developed, called the *bijuli dekchi*, which can be used for boiling water and cooking rice and lentils in a similar way to traditional cooking stoves.

Other aspects of energy services

Technology choice is not the only thing that must be considered when providing energy services. The service provided must be affordable to the user, in terms of both initial investment costs and daily running costs. Often a change of energy source will involve an investment by the user, which may either be beyond the means of the user, or may place a substantial strain on the user's income. Often the perception of the risk is increased by the uncertainty that a new technology will be reliable in meeting the user's needs.

Innovative approaches to providing affordable energy services may have to be sought. For example, the technology to use the energy service could be leased to the user, instead of being sold. This way the overall risk to the user is reduced. Alternatively, innovative credit and tariff schemes may be employed, in particular to extend the energy service to the poorest in the village. These options are covered in greater detail in other chapters.

Other considerations of the energy service provided may include initial training in the use and safety aspects of the technology, and the provision of maintenance services. Without these additional services, the energy technology may not effectively serve the energy service required. This is illustrated by a recent initiative in Zimbabwe, which aimed to overcome the main problems that previous projects had suffered in establishing photovoltaic pumping systems. After studying existing PV programmes, the Zimbabwe Department of Energy and the German agency GTZ found that two key aspects of failure were the lack of training for the users and the absence of specialized repair and maintenance services within the financial reach of the local community.

Energy service survey guide

People in village

The objective is to identify the types of village people and their numbers, so that every grouping is included in the study, including minority and marginalized groups.

- men with farms; men without farms
- women with cash incomes; women with no cash income
- average number of children per household
- elderly people
- disadvantaged groups (disabled, chronically ill, extremely poor)
- professionals (teachers, medics, officials)
- people who spend only part of the year in the village

- visitors/tourists
- what are the main activities of each group of people?
- have there been any changes in the population, people moving into or out of the village, and why?

Village institution
This creates a list of the institutions that may be involved with an energy project. What are their capabilities, length of experience and status in the village?

- private enterprises
- societies
- banks
- government offices
- voluntary organizations/NGOs
- religious communities
- technical workshops

Energy patterns in the village
This identifies current energy use patterns, including fuel use, and expected future energy needs:

- types of fuel used (wood, dung, kerosene, etc.)?
- what are the constraints to accessing these fuels – access, cost, labour for collection, difficulties in using the fuels?
- what are the prospects for electric grid connection?
- what benefit would a new energy source provide for the village?
- what changes in the energy pattern are expected in the next five years?

Village organizations
It is important to identify the way the village organizes itself to carry out its daily business. To do this, identify the following features:

- types of organization: welfare societies, farmers' associations, government projects, woman's groups, business organizations
- how long has the organization been running?
- has it been successful?
- how are these organizations managed? Do they keep accounts?
- could the organization take on activities relating to a new energy scheme?

Household and individual surveys
Carry out more detailed surveys to make sure you have identified patterns of energy use particular to the area. The following points should be covered:

- size of household, ages, and occupations
- cash income, non-cash income, and farm produce
- amount of land, livestock, tools
- current energy use patterns – traditional and commercial energy sources
- desire for new energy source

- how much can they afford to pay for energy services?
- how would the new energy services affect the members of the household: men, women, children, elderly?
- will the household energy demands change in the next five years?
- are there any concerns about using new energy services?

Entrepreneurs and local business
It is important to identify uses of energy that generate income in the community. Gather information to determine:

- current energy service needs for various businesses in the village
- the capacity of the business to adopt new energy options or develop new business based on the new energy source. How much energy would be required?
- what business practices exist in the village: record-keeping for finances and maintenance, means of tariff collection, conflict resolution, employment practice, extending benefits of the business to marginalized groups?
- would the new energy source have a negative impact on the business, such as diverting customers elsewhere, loss of jobs, and so on?
- how much would business pay for new energy services?
- could the business run and manage the new energy service: who would employ the operators, keep accounts, maintain spare parts inventory, collect tariffs, etc?

Village Service
Some communities will already have common uses of energy (such as communications or refrigeration at a clinic). What energy needs do they have now, and what energy services are required for:

- school?
- clinic?

Other village schemes
Finally, it is important to ensure that the provision of energy services is coordinated with other developments within the community and in the area. In particular, identify:

- what other development schemes are occurring in the village
- similar energy schemes in neighbouring villages.

Outputs of the survey
The survey should result in a report, to include:

- a map of the village, showing households and productive and commercial activities
- a summary of the type of people in the village
- a list of the village institutions, organizations and village leaders

- a report of current energy resource management and future village plans for development of energy resources
- summaries of notes from interviews, indicating energy service needs and willingness to pay for these
- a sector-by-sector breakdown of energy service requirements (type and quantity of energy required) in the village
- an assessment of the potential for extending new energy services to the marginalized groups in the community
- an assessment of the capability of the local organizations or entrepreneurs to manage a new village energy project (technical capabilities, financial knowledge, and management skills)
- an assessment of the village organizational and management systems, to review their ability to raise capital for the project, to collect tariffs, to arrange maintenance, etc.

(Adapted from the Capability and demand survey in the *Micro-hydro Design Manual: A guide to small-scale water power schemes*, A. Harvey et al., IT Publications, London, 1993)

Participatory and co-operative planning and management of rural electricity supplies

Rural populations do not normally receive their electricity supply from national grids. Rural areas are often supplied either by local mini-grids or by stand-alone

Rural populations do not normally receive their electricity supply from national grids

systems, such as small diesel generating sets. Informal settlements in urban areas of developing countries are also unlikely to receive grid electricity.

In rural communities and informal urban settlements, payments for electricity from single consumers are so low that they are not cost-effective for a utility to manage. In such situations, co-operatives can function as aggregate bodies for low-income households, or can own generation resources and distribution networks.

This section examines the ways in which co-operative and participatory management and ownership can increase the access that rural communities have to electricity supplies. The adoption of participatory approaches involving communities in the whole process (i.e. planning, installation, implementation, monitoring, and the operation and maintenance of the scheme) has proved to have positive impacts with respect to community self-confidence and empowerment.

Approaches to rural electrification

Supply-driven approaches

The governments of most less-developed countries have electrification programmes that aim to reach rural areas. Rural electrification is an issue upon which local election campaigns are often based, and is often cited as a priority for rural populations, ranking higher than road extension and local provision of health care. In general, national electrification programmes are viewed as a development in national infrastructure, and as such are centrally planned. They generally involve high levels of investment, and are based on an increase in generation capacity and the extension of transmission grids. Such programmes are largely supply driven: the generation phase is planned and rural communities are connected as and when the grid reaches them. Demand assessments for such rural electrification programmes are likely to be based upon assessments of community size, linked to national standard consumption configurations. Participative approaches are not common.

In general, national grid extension programmes have been found to proceed at a pace that does not meet the growth in demand. In the worst cases, they do not keep pace even with the growth in population. The cost of electricity produced by conventional power stations is usually lower than that produced at small decentralized installations.

Nationally set tariff rates for grid-delivered power often do not reflect the true cost of electricity delivered. In the rural areas of developing countries, consumers often expect to pay no more for grid electricity than do their urban counterparts. This attitude can also affect rural electrification programmes based on decentralized generation, where consumers view electricity as a state-controlled and regulated service, and refuse to accept that the tariff they pay should reflect the true cost of energy production.

Demand-led approaches

In countries where 100 per cent of the population does not have access to the grid, centrally planned rural electrification programmes often operate in parallel with entrepreneurial electrification developments. In the remote areas of some countries, local business owners offer electric lighting and battery charging based on a variety of small-scale generation technologies. Such schemes are generally demand led (i.e. market led), are completely commercial and receive no subsidy from national-level bodies. They do not, however, reach all rural communities. Within a rural community, fractions of the population can also be excluded from electricity services, usually by economic factors.

Programmes that facilitate appropriate changes in policy structures at national level, and institutional capacity strengthening for intermediary bodies (such as rural electrification commissions, rural energy co-ordinating bodies, electrification cooperative associations and energy forums) can greatly increase the level of activity in the entrepreneurial energy supply sector, allowing wider access to electricity supplies in rural areas. In particular, policy and strategy changes are required which facilitate the development of more numerous communal schemes with a variety of ownership and management structures.

Demand-led approaches meet existing needs and desires, so to target these, an element of consultation with the 'market' or 'target group' is required. It is important to note that 'consultation' is not the same as 'participation'. Participation takes the idea of involving the target group one step further, so that they have genuine control over the process of planning and managing their own energy supply. Participative approaches to development, originating in the areas of agriculture and natural resource management, have therefore incorporated participation into the design of the consultation process, the process of consultation itself, the analysis and assessment phase, and into the resulting project design, implementation and subsequent management. The next section reviews participative approaches and their application in the field of rural electrification.

Participation and development

Participatory approaches to development are based on the idea that the people who are the focus of the investigation, implementation or analysis know more about their lives and environment, and what they need to improve their quality of life, than the professionals who are working with them. Teams using participatory approaches generally seek the minimum level of information necessary to address an issue or problem, use several different sources of information, and follow investigation, analysis and planning procedures that reflect the experience of the culture in which they are working.

Participatory planning of electricity supplies

In development work related to agriculture and natural resources, the needs and practices of the local community can be used as a strong indicator of practices and techniques that will gain support and be adopted in a community in a sustainable manner. The level of technical knowledge required to carry out an identical process for an electrification scheme is not found in the general population of any country, developing or otherwise.

Electrification schemes can in fact be designed and installed only by trained engineers; financing can be gained only by economically sound propositions; and trained operators and managers are required to ensure scheme performance. The participative approaches described above therefore need some modification in order to allow the involvement of stakeholders outside the immediate user community. Consultation can take place in the process of demand assessment and load planning, ownership and financing models, and management and operation.

One way to do this is via a process of consultation involving an intermediary organization which identifies and consults scheme stakeholders in order to identify constraints on decentralized rural electrification and the actions needed to overcome those constraints. While this intermediary body can be formed in part from representatives of the user community, others must be involved in order to ensure scheme viability in other sectors.

Co-operative ownership and management of schemes
Electrification schemes controlled by the scheme users are usually initiated in communities where a supply system has not previously existed. Poorer communities in developing countries cannot generally afford electricity, and may have other priorities (such as clean water supplies, or road access to the nearest urban centre). Community-controlled electricity supply schemes therefore often exist in communities that are relatively affluent, in comparison with those that have, for example, community-controlled water supplies.

Participative planning can contribute to scheme sustainability

14

Despite this relative wealth, user groups are rarely rich, and are often established in regions where there are problems with the step-up in the capability (technical and managerial) required for scheme management. This is exacerbated in countries (such as Nepal) where there are no established business units other than the family or the individual. User groups involved in electricity provision can own the generation capability as well as distribution networks. This occurs at all levels of scale.

Scale
Levels of user involvement generally vary with the scale of the utility scheme in question, although ownership and management frameworks also have some impact on this. Scale also affects scheme viability and may have effects, due to the fact that the higher costs of larger projects may encourage external ownership and exclude local owners.

The contribution of community groups in general becomes less as the scale of utility projects increases. Existing local management institutions become less relevant and there is a greater need for the construction of new ownership and management structures. This is particularly the case for electricity supply cooperatives, where there is some need for technical management capability.

In larger projects, community management is more likely to occur at a later stage in project development. This increases the danger of not identifying local needs and increases the risk that the community may have less commitment to, and understanding of, the project.

Models of ownership
The following represents one way of categorizing groups involved in user-controlled electricity provision.

Village electrification committee. In this case, the supply scheme concerned is quite small scale and supplies a few hundred households at most. The committee owns the electric power distribution system and is set up so that it represents the community population. The way in which it does this is determined by many factors, including:

○ local custom
○ legal requirements, and
○ grant or loan conditions.

Representation on the committee is by virtue of election, leadership status or role within the community. In practice, such committees often reflect the hierarchy of their community of origin, but are generally found to be more sustainable if they represent all sections of the population.

The committee is likely to be involved in scheme planning and implementation, and in overseeing revenue collection, billing and operation and maintenance. In the case of electricity, the user group can either own the generation plant that produces the electricity or buy the power in bulk from a generating company and distribute it to the community. The committee's day-to-day

Village electrification committees are often formally constituted and supported by rural development initiatives

Photograph: Intermediate Technology/Ann Watts

responsibilities will also reflect the source of the electricity it distributes. This type of group is likely to involve maximum personal commitment and activity levels on the part of the users.

Regional user organization. At this level, groups supplying electricity are likely to be bodies buying power from a larger company and distributing it, as above.

Such bodies require a moderate level of personal commitment from users. In practice, these are likely to be involved only at the scheme inception and when problems occur. Day-to-day activities will be delegated to a small cadre of members.

Large-scale utility. Members of such groups (often state-registered co-operatives), perceive little difference in electricity provision from the group and from a 'normal' utility. Although users are members of the group by virtue of their receipt of supply, there is little personal commitment and activity.

Other models also exist, and overlap the boundaries of the above sets to some extent. For example, a locally dominated shareholder company generates and distributes its own power in Salleri Chialsa in Nepal. This is technically a private company, but shares in the company denote a degree of representation (i.e. voting rights) rather than a tradable commodity.

Conclusions

Many imaginative management and ownership options have been developed for rural electrification schemes (See case study 1 on the *Chalan micro-hydro scheme* in Peru for instance, or the reference to community ownership in case study 5 on *Electric cooking with micro-hydro power* in Nepal.

Ownership and management options can be adapted and developed as locally appropriate but care should be taken that inappropriate ownership and management structures are not imposed on consumer communities. In order to bridge the gap between the technical, financial, implementation and management areas, it is necessary for participative work to be carried out with all scheme stakeholders via a consultation process. If possible, this should be facilitated by a neutral intermediary body which would ideally have the confidence of the technical and financial communities in addition to that of the consumer community.

2

Financing energy supplies for rural communities

Financing options

Many studies show that the key constraint to energy supply for rural communities is access to the initial capital needed to buy the equipment to harness the resource. This leads rural communities to choose energy options that are cheap on a day-to-day basis, but which offer a poor quality of energy supply and are expensive over the longer term.

There are also other barriers which prevent rural communities from choosing efficient and cost-effective energy options. Institutional aspects, infrastructure, and access to technical and other support, for instance, must all be taken into consideration in rural energy policies. This chapter provides a review of the instruments available, and answers key questions related to their implementation.

Grants

Principles and mechanisms

Grants may appear to be the least expensive source of funding for the recipient. However, lessons from the projects funded entirely on a grant basis show poor quality of management, maintenance, and lack of responsibility from the beneficiaries. For example, hundreds of grant-funded PV systems were installed in the Pacific Islands (Tonga, Papua New Guinea, Fiji, Marshal Islands), but there was no mechanism to manage or maintain the schemes or to collect the fees on a regular basis. When centralized government bodies were responsible for maintenance and its implementation, the system did not work properly because of long delays and high costs for repairs. Eventually, the systems were either abandoned or are working at a fraction of the initial capacity. There are no cases in which systems are working according to the design. On the other hand, it appears that projects carried out in the same region are successful when they are managed and maintained by owners through co-operatives and with fees collected regularly.

Subsidies

Principles and mechanisms

Generally speaking, subsidies are granted either to services, commodities, or activities that are viewed by governments as crucial to the livelihood of low-income people (transport, energy, health, food) or to maintain economic sectors viewed as strategic, such as agriculture, defence, etc.

Subsidies occur when the sales do not cover the cost of production or imports. For example, in most developing countries some types of energy are subsidized either directly or indirectly (e.g. kerosene, electricity for rural areas, etc.). All governments transfer resources from some groups of people within an economy to others in the belief that to do so is to improve the well-being of the society and the way its economy operates. It does this for reasons of equity or because it believes that the market allocation of resources does not adequately result in the best interest of the society.

Subsidies can either be direct, such as payments that reduce the costs of inputs to an investment, or indirect, such as changes in prices, taxes, and the provision of recurrent inputs such as training or the provision of infrastructure. In addition, subsidies can be intended or unintended. This latter category can be a very large component of any country's subsidy regime, for instance when the losses of an enterprise are written off by the government (e.g. electricity with utilities) or where loans are not to be repaid by borrowers. These tend to be indiscriminate and can often favour people other than the target group. Inflation can also have unpredictable effects, as the amount borrowed can reduce rapidly in real terms if inflation is high and the loan is not index-linked.

Side effects of subsidies
Much of the logic of the subsidy rests on the assumption that there will be a supply response. Many forms of subsidy are known to have side-effects that are harmful to more self-sustaining development in the longer term or do not reach the intended beneficiaries. For instance, the current support to fossil fuels makes it very difficult for many renewable sources of energy to compete. The subsidy to LPG in some West African countries is benefiting the middle- and higher income families who can afford gas cookers. When subsidies are granted to imported products, the development of local production may be hindered. This is the case in the agricultural sector and increasingly in the sector of renewable energy such as photovoltaic.

Credit

Principles and mechanisms
Credit is a financial intermediation between economic agents with credit and those with deficit. For various reasons (confidence, pooling the resources of several small lenders, skills, etc.) an intermediary – generally a financial institution – is necessary to implement the financial link between the two agents. In the agricultural sector, because of the gap between the income when the crops are sold and the expenses, various forms of credit were developed to support both poor and wealthy farmers. However, the types of credit widely used in the agriculture sector are not suitable for funding rural energy schemes for poor communities, particularly when the pay-back period is spread over a medium-term period. The costs of recovering small loans in isolated areas are fairly high. Most of the banks do not have the experience to deal with rural credit for small or micro schemes. Because of the risk, banks are inclined to impose guarantees that poor rural communities have difficulty meeting. For example in Sri Lanka a

19

typical loan for a photovoltaic system may cover up to the 80 per cent of the cost over a period of five years but the interest is relatively high and the bank requires guarantees from the borrower. Participatory planning techniques can be useful in situations such as these, where it is vital that all stakeholders fully understand each other and their objectives.

Loans are a relatively new concept in financing energy supply for rural communities and they are often implemented by NGOs or co-operatives which provide the guarantees requested by the financial institutions. Loans, even with subsidized interest rates, provide a minimum of guarantees that communities are interested in the acquisition of a particular technology and the maintenance of the scheme. Various ways have been used to grant loans and to pay back the loans.

Rural electrification schemes in Peru can be financed using revolving funds

Photograph: Intermediate Technology/Steve Fisher

In Peru, for example, the organization Intermediate Technology is implementing a project which provides loans to organizations in rural areas for setting up micro-hydroelectric power plants. The loan is granted from a 'revolving fund', a fund that is set up to lend for a specific purpose, and which re-lends the money for further micro-hydro schemes as the previous loans are paid back. The interest on the loan covers the cost of administering the scheme. The fund is a joint initiative of Intermediate Technology in Peru and the Inter-American Development Bank, and loans are given only to projects that have passed technical and economic criteria. Loans are also accompanied by training and technical assistance.

Through the project, three micro-hydroelectric power plants have been set up so far, with four more under construction. Each of the installed plants benefits more than 250 families. Of the first three loans provided, one has already been

20

recovered. The programme has been specifically designed to impact on very poor communities through subsidies from RENON (the Regional Government of the Northeast Maranon Region), as well as to benefit the small-scale rural producers who gain direct access to credit. The programme has introduced innovations in areas such as the use of PVC pipes, locally manufactured electromechanical equipment, and various civil works construction techniques.

In the case of photovoltaic systems, where the beneficiaries are very often individuals, credit is granted on individual basis. Various forms of loan have been developed and, generally speaking, interest rates for these loans are below normal commercial rates. For example, in Rwanda the Union des Banques Populaire du Rwanda, with more than 100 branches in rural areas, has offered credit at a low interest rate (9 per cent) spread over a period of 12 to 36 months. In order to access a loan, however, the borrower must have savings in the bank of up to 20 per cent of the total cost of the equipment.

Another formula adopted in the Philippines is a loan limited to the cost of the PV panels, whose life expectancy is far beyond the duration of the loan. In case of non-payment, the bank can take back the panels. Experience shows that rural households find the resources to fund the batteries and the lamps. The rate of loan repayment is fairly high because the bank may repossess the panels in order to recover the loan.

Financing rural community energy schemes (A combination of various funding sources and instruments)

Increasingly, the common pattern for financing rural energy schemes involves a range of types of funding such as grants, subsidies, loans, contributions in kind. The following example from Nepal gives a good idea of this trend.

The 25kW micro-hydro plant located in the village of Muktinath (Mustang district) was funded by USAID and Intermediate Technology, a loan from the Agricultural Development Bank of Nepal, and a contribution from the village (see breakdown in Figure 2.1).

The loan (which includes an interest rate of 14 per cent) was to be paid in eight instalments over eight years, but was in fact cleared before the deadline. The beneficiaries, who are the owners, contributed towards labour and transportation of the materials. Around 98 households in the Purang district benefit from the scheme. This includes 12 lodges for tourists (trekkers), who represent a good source of income for the community.

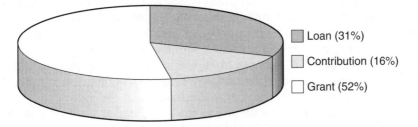

Loan (31%)
Contribution (16%)
Grant (52%)

Figure 2.1: *Financing breakdown for the Muktinath micro-hydro scheme in Nepal*

Micro-hydro schemes are often financed using a combination of financing instruments

Photograph: Intermediate Technology

The scheme is managed by 11 members from the community who form the electricity management committee that decides, among other things, the tariff rate at which power will be made available to users. The charge at the time of writing is Rp.0.25/W/month (equivalent to US$0.06/W/month at March 1998 currency rates). The users pay a fixed tariff based on the capacity of their supply. Their supply is limited, using simple and cheap current limiting devices, and the scheme therefore avoids the use of electricity meters, which are very expensive.

Financial performance

Financial performance is one of the fundamental factors to be considered when selecting energy options for rural villages. Although there may be non-financial benefits with particular technologies, such as environmental gains, improved environmental health aspects, or greater social benefits, it is often the financial performance of the technology that is the deciding factor. There must be consideration of the upfront capital costs, the daily running and fuel costs, annual maintenance costs, and any income generated from selling the energy. To compare the overall costs and benefits of the various options for supplying energy needs, it is essential to make a detailed financial analysis of each option.

This is necessary for two reasons:

○ to compare the various options in financial terms, and

○ to ensure that the energy project is financially viable.

This section explains some of the financial terminology involved, and describes various methods of financial analysis for comparing the energy options.

Financial terminology

The capital cost of an energy project includes all the upfront costs, from project conception to commissioning the technology. These will include all costs for:

○ project management, design, and engineering

○ equipment costs, including transport of equipment to the site, and

○ installation costs, including any housing or mounting for the technology.

Capital costs of energy technologies will vary from location to location, depending on the local availability of the technology, the distance equipment must be transported, whether the equipment has been imported or manufactured locally, and so on. Capital costs will often be covered partially or fully by a bank loan, on which interest must be paid.

Annual operating costs will include the staffing, fuel, maintenance, and repair costs for operating the energy technology. Most of these costs will be predictable and fairly constant each year. The most unpredictable operating cost will be for repairs to unexpected damage or breakdown of the technology. Provision must be made for unexpected repairs.

Project lifetime is very important when comparing energy options. Some technologies, such as a micro-hydro plant or solar panels, will have a lifetime of over 20 years. Other technologies, such as diesel generators, will have to be refurbished or replaced after less than 10 years. The financial cost of refurbishment or replacement of the technology during the project lifetime must be included in any financial comparison of technologies.

For any energy supply, the most cost-effective technology is usually chosen to harness the energy resources available. The apparent cost effectiveness of a particular technology can vary considerably, however, depending on the way in which it is calculated. Technologies that have a low initial capital cost may be very expensive to run because of high fuel prices. This is common with conventional fossil fuel technology. On the other hand, the experience with many renewable energy technologies is that the initial capital investment in often relatively high, but the running costs are very low.

The *efficiency* of the technology affects both capital and running costs. The efficiency is the ratio of the useful energy output to the energy input (in the form of fuel, sunlight, hydro, or wind potential). More efficient technologies often have a higher capital cost, because they require higher precision engineering. For commercial fuel technologies, however, more efficient technologies will save on fuel costs.

The *load factor* of an energy technology will significantly affect the revenue collected from an energy supply scheme. The load factor of an installed energy technology can be defined as the energy used in a year expressed as a percentage of the energy that could have been produced if the plant had operated at full output all the time. Ideally, an energy scheme should be planned to have a high load factor, so that maximum revenue can be collected from the energy sold, and equipment performance can be kept as constant as possible.

The load factor will be low if:

o the plant capacity is oversized for the actual load required by the community
o the energy demand is only during a short period of the day or year, or
o the energy technology breaks down frequently during the year.

Therefore, when planning an energy project, it is essential also to plan for optimum loading patterns across the day and all year round. A load survey will be necessary to predict loading patterns and the required plant capacity (see the section on Energy services in Chapter 1).

Financial indicators

Unit costs of energy

To ascertain which technology option produces energy most cheaply, the cost of producing one unit of energy from each option should be estimated. In addition, this will set the minimum charge that can be made for selling the energy allowing for all the production costs to be covered.

The unit costs are equal to the total annual costs divided by the annual number of units supplied.

$$\text{Unit energy costs} = \frac{\text{total annual costs}}{\text{energy supplied per year}}$$

The annual costs will include the operation and maintenance costs (O+M) plus the annual cost of the capital spent on the plant (C_{annual}). C_{annual} may be the annual repayment on the capital loan. The energy supplied will be equal to the maximum energy that the plant can produce in a year (E_{max}) times the predicted load factor (LF).

For example, a 10kW hydro power plant, which has a loan repayment of $2000 per year and annual operation costs of $200, has total annual costs of $2200. If it is expected that the plant will be used for only three hours per day for lighting, then the load factor of the plant will be 12.5 per cent. The total number of units sold per year will be 10 950kWh. Therefore the unit energy cost will be: $0.2/kWh.

If there was a daytime load that used the energy supplied for a further four hours a day, the plant factor would be doubled, and the unit cost of production halved.

A projection for the unit cost of various electricity technologies is given in Figure 2.2, in US cents per electrical unit. Although actual unit costs will vary from location to location, the figure indicates the general pattern expected over the 15-year period to 2010. In this figure, it can be seen that the photovoltaic option is the most expensive. However, the capital cost of PV cells is expected to decrease significantly by 2010, which will then make the unit cost for PV similar to that of other technology options.

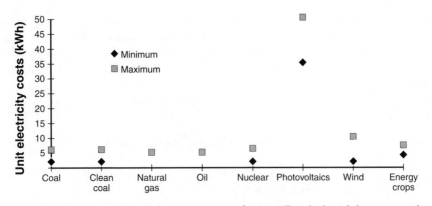

Figure 2.2: *Unit costs for various sources of centralized electricity generation*

Simple payback period

Another factor that will concern an investor will be the period in which the investment will be paid back. The simple payback period calculation will give a quick estimate of this period:

$$\text{Simple payback} = \frac{\text{total capital cost}}{\text{annual revenue} - \text{annual operation cost}}$$

For example, if the total capital cost of a wind plant is \$40 000, annual income from selling energy is \$16 000 and annual costs are \$3000, then the simple payback period is:

$$\frac{40\,000}{16\,000 - 3000} = 3 \text{ years}$$

This calculation does not consider that the value of money changes over time, or that there is to be interest paid on the loan. It therefore has to be used as a very rough estimate, rather than an actual calculation of payback period. This indicator is often used by bankers as a guide to payback, particularly for smaller loans.

Value of money over time

Money is generally regarded as having a 'time value'. This reflects the fact that possessing a certain amount of money in the present allows someone to carry out activities which could generate them more money in the future. It also reflects the fact that \$1000 will purchase less in one year's time than it can purchase today. In general, the 'value' of a certain amount of money (i.e. its purchasing power) is therefore said to decrease over time.

If the value, of money is worth 10 per cent less in one year's time, it could be said that $1000 in one year's time will be worth the equivalent of $909 today. This is called discounting to present value, with a discount rate of 10 per cent in this case.

To find the present value of a sum of money in a number of years' time the general equation is:

$$\text{Present value} = \frac{\text{Future value}}{(1+r)^n}$$

where n is the number of years in the future that the sum will arise, and r is the discount rate.

So that, for example, if I have $1000 in three years' time, with a discount rate of 10 per cent, its present value will be:

$$\frac{1000}{(1+0.1)^3} = \$751$$

Of course, the discount rate has to be estimated for these calculations. The choice of discount rate will depend on the value given to future sums of money, and may be the user's own selected discount rate based on the user's own value of future sums of money.

Using a high discount rate will bias against projects that have a high capital expenditure, but low annual costs (such as most renewable technologies), and will be more favourable to projects with low capital costs but high fuel costs (such as fossil fuel technologies). This is because future costs will appear small in comparison to current costs.

The annuity equation
An energy scheme, of course, will have recurring costs and income each year. Therefore, it will be necessary to sum all the costs and incomes over the years. The present value of the total net income (revenue minus operational costs) is found by using the annuity equation.

If we assume that net income is a fixed sum of money per year, it is possible to find the present value of the total income over a number of years. The fixed annual sum is called the annuity.

To find the present value of the total sum of the annuity (A) over a number of years, we use the annuity equations. (See References and Resources for further details.)

$$\text{Total present value} = \frac{A \times \{ (1+r)^n - 1 \}}{r(1+r)^n} = A \times \text{discount factor}$$

For example, with a discount rate of 12 per cent, an annual income of $1000 for 15 years will have a total present value of $6800. This shows that an annual income of $1000 over 15 years is the equivalent to having $6800 at the present time, when a discount rate of 12 per cent is assumed.

Net present value
The net present value (NPV) is the sum of all the revenue minus all the capital and operating costs in terms of present values. At a decided discount rate of r%

this is expressed as NPV(r%). To produce a first estimate of NPV we assume that the annual net income of a project is a fixed sum over the project lifetime. We can then calculate the present value of the total net income using the annuity equation above. Therefore, NPV is equal to the present value (PV) of net income minus the capital cost (C) of the plant:

$$NPV = PV - C$$

So, using the above example of present value of net income, which is equivalent to $6800 at a discount rate of 12 per cent, if the capital cost of the energy project was $5500, then NPV= $1300. This example assumes that the expense of the capital cost occurs right at the beginning of the project.

Internal rate of return

The internal rate of return (IRR) is the value of the discount rate, r, at which the NPV equals zero. That is, the discount rate at which total income equals total costs at present values. This can be found by an iterative process of trying various values of r until the equation equals zero. It is made simpler if the above table of discount factors for annuities is used, or a more common practice now is to use spreadsheets for very rapid calculation of IRR. Projects that have the best financial performance will have a higher IRR.

To find the IRR in the above example, the present value of net income would have to equal $5500 for NPV = 0. We would then go back to the annuity equation and substitute values for r until the present value equals $5500. This occurs at approximately r = 16 per cent. Therefore, in the above example, IRR = 16 per cent.

Variable annual costs and revenue

It should be noted that the above examples all make the assumption that the annual net income is a fixed sum each year. This approach is useful for making an initial estimate of the financial performance for a pre-feasibility study. This assumption is, however, very unrealistic. It is more likely that both costs and revenue will vary from year to year. For a more accurate estimate of NPV and IRR it will be essential to estimate the real value of net income for each year of the project, then calculate the present value for each year individually. The sum of the present values for each year will give the total present value of net income.

In addition, for some energy projects the technology will have to be refurbished or replaced after a number of years of operation. This will mean a large cost in that year. This should also be taken into account when calculating present values.

Policy and market instruments

The private sector can be encouraged to engage in the provision of energy supply services by the construction of 'market instruments'. These may take the form of tax incentives, or import duty waivers/concessions or competitive tenders for private generation for grid-connected generation schemes or for decentralized power supply.

They overlap strongly with 'policy instruments', which, in this context, are taken to mean policy structures that favour the development of rural energy supply options by any actor, including state bodies and parastatal organizations. Policy instruments can take the form of support for non-conventional energy supply options, community management and participation, the development of appropriate low-cost supply standards (e.g. low-cost electricity supply options), the deregulation of electricity supply systems below a certain limit, and so on. The instruments are outlined below, and linked to the ways in which they can be used to support the development of rural energy supply options.

Tax incentives and import duty concessions

These can take the form of a waiver of import duties for imported equipment destined for rural energy supply purposes. Differential rates for renewable energy equipment to reduce the cost relative to equipment for fossil fuel burning equipment may also be used to encourage reduction of dependence on these fuels.

For example, several countries currently operate favourable Tax conditions for new Renewable Energy (RE) generation schemes, in particular:

- *Depreciation*: Where developers are allowed to accelerate the depreciation of RE equipment, this offsets the high up-front costs of RE developments. High depreciation rates therefore provide an investment incentive. This policy instrument is used, for example, in India. This instrument could also be applied to bodies carrying out, say, rural electrification or biogas supply programmes.
- *Tax holidays*: In the same way, tax holidays on income generated by RE schemes are used worldwide as an investment incentive, to offset the capital-intensive nature of RE. Such instruments can also be used where rural entrepreneurs install rural energy supply schemes.
- *Environmental impact taxing structures*: Countries and states can operate favourable taxing structures for RE which take into account the fact that such generation options have lower environmental impacts than generation from fossil fuels. For instance, the much-discussed 'carbon tax' could be seen as an inverted tax break for RE developments. Such schemes, (together with the use of emissions trading schemes such as the Clean Development Mechanism proposed at the Kyoto Summit), could also be to the benefit of rural energy supply schemes.
- *Targeted subsidies*: States can set up subsidy schemes that favour one energy source over others. In some countries, for instance, the price of LPG is significantly reduced by government subsidy. In others, petrol can be taxed at high rates to increase its price to the user.

Supply contracts

Governments may decide to allocate the provision of electricity or other energy services to the private sector. They may wish to maintain some control over the planning process, however, and do this through the competitive awarding of contracts for the supply of energy to particular regions. Companies may be invited to come up with their own proposals for particular schemes (e.g. small hydro, biomass, solar, or diesel). The call for proposals may be based on inviting proposals for the supply of electricity for a particular region, or from particular sources, and evaluating them against the soundness of the proposed methodology, the costs, and the experience of the company. In the case of grid-connected schemes, a purchase price for electrical energy may be agreed, based on the 'firm' power able to be supplied by the generator. This price may vary depending on the season, the source, or the time of day. For example, it may be advantageous to incorporate some water storage in a hydro scheme, if a better price will be paid for electricity at particular times of day (peak demand).

In the case of decentralized electricity generation, concessions for the supply of electricity to a particular region may be awarded by competitive tender. The obligation for the national utility company to supply particular areas of low population and low demand is removed, and the ownership of existing decentralized electrification facilities, and the authorization, even obligation, to develop new facilities and to sell the electricity to the consumers, is awarded to a company by competitive tender. The prime consideration in awarding such contracts could be the lowest cost to provide a particular level of service. The technical standards for the supply of electricity, the availability of the supply, and the tariffs charged to the consumer are defined in the contractual agreement.

On the other hand, the prime consideration used to decide between companies tendering for the supply contract could be the likelihood that the supply would be sustainable. This could then take into account local issues and information that can be determined only in a participatory manner, making it likely that a locally owned and managed company wins the contract to supply its own power.

Cost reduction measures for electricity

The costs of supplying these electrical services to remote areas may be higher than for areas of higher population density. They may also exceed the projected income from the consumers.

This can be compensated for in part by a reduced level of supply (e.g. hours of availability, lower maximum demand), but it may be that the government wishes to limit the cost to the consumer to a level lower than that which would be needed to provide an adequate return for the producer. In fact, the government may want to regulate the behaviour of these companies by limiting the profit levels to an agreed amount, and also limiting the tariffs that can be charged, particularly for the consumers with the lower levels of demand. This may require a level of subsidy for the smaller consumers – i.e. a subsidy level that can be claimed by the generator to match the revenues collected from the consumers. The tariffs in these cases would increase with the level of demand – i.e. the tariff would increase in blocks – e.g. the first 30kW at a low tariff, the next 30kW at a higher tariff, and above 60kW, where the highest tariff would apply. The cost of supplying the smaller consumers may be reduced by various means, such as prepayment metering, fixed maximum demand tariffs with current limiters, and supply limited to certain hours in the day.

Low demand density in rural areas is a major challenge to energy scheme development

Photograph: Intermediate Technology/Lindel Caine

Load limited electricity supply

The marginal cost of conventional metering-and-tariff connection is far too high for many low-income households. In order to overcome this constraint, a favourable option is that of the 'load limited supply'. Such supplies attract a capacity tariff, with the consumer being charged a fixed monthly fee (according to the load limit) irrespective of the total amount of energy consumed. The household does not have a costly meter, but is equipped with a load limiting device.

Load limiters work by limiting, to an agreed amount, the current supplied to the consumer. If the current exceeds this value the device automatically disconnects the supply. Some types of load limiter must be reset manually, while others automatically reset when the overload is removed. Such supply options are often best marketed as 'economy' or 'unmetered', in order to overcome the negative connotations of 'limited' supplies.

The main advantages of load limited supplies are:

○ low revenue collection costs
○ reduced costs of transmission, distribution, and generation
○ low initial capital cost
○ cash up front for the electricity utility, and
○ easier budgeting of payments by consumer.

The main disadvantages of load limiters are:

○ increased opportunities for fraud and theft

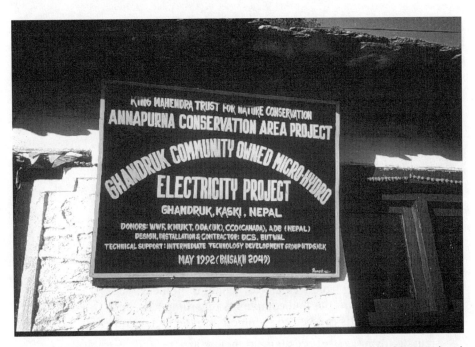

The Ghandruk community-owned scheme in Nepal uses load limiting technology as part of its demand management

Photograph: Intermediate Technology/Steve Fisher

- o poor reliability
- o restricted electricity usage
- o poor accuracy, and
- o uneconomical use of electricity.

Prefabricated wiring systems

House-wiring is a major expense that can deter households from subscribing to a connection. The labour costs for conventional wiring are especially high for houses of traditional construction where installation is difficult. A solution to this problem is the use of low-cost versatile house-wiring systems. These come in two forms; wiring harnesses and 'ready boards'. Conventional wiring systems, as used in the West, are too expensive and inflexible for low-income households in some countries.

In some countries, extensions to house-wiring are frequent. When families get bigger or their income improves, they normally extend their homes rather than move. Hence, even if the initial wiring is installed to a high standard, the extensions can be wired by unqualified people. Safe and versatile house-wiring systems are required to meet these conditions.

Wiring harnesses reduce house-wiring costs significantly and allow lights and sockets to be repositioned. They are ideal for consumers who use just one or two lights and perhaps a radio. 'Ready boards' are significantly more expensive than wiring harnesses, but are suitable for households that have a range of appliances, or use high-current devices.

Prepayment meters

Prepayment meters require the consumer to purchase units of electricity from the supply authority in advance. With most existing systems, the consumer purchases a magnetic card which has a number of units recorded on it. The consumer inserts this into their meter, which then records the new units as credits. The meter then automatically cancels the code on the card so that it cannot be reused. The meter displays the total number of credits available and, depending upon the make, may also indicate the rate of consumption and/or provide warnings when the credits are almost exhausted. The advantages of the prepayment meter include:

- no meter reading required
- no billing required
- prepayment means no overdue accounts and no disconnection and reconnection costs
- easy budgeting by the consumer and the ability to pay for small amounts in the same way that kerosene is purchased
- no costs resulting from a change of tenant or home owner
- no consumer enquiries and complaints regarding bills, and
- time of day tariffs can be programmed into the meter and easily modified.

The main disadvantages of prepayment meters are the:

- high cost of the meter, and
- the need for a well-organized sales/support service.

Prepayment meters have been used extensively in South Africa during the past few years. They are used principally in the townships and are fitted along with ready boards, as described above. The meters cost the utility approximately $90 each.

Prepayment metering technology is developing quite rapidly. Remote metering systems are being developed that enable meter reading, crediting of prepayments, and disconnection/reconnection to be carried out by communications over the distribution network. These systems could be cheaper than the more conventional prepayment systems, both in terms of hardware and running costs. While the technology of remote metering systems already exists, it is likely to be adopted only as utilities upgrade their current equipment, which will probably happen only over the next decade or so.

Revised safety standards

Several issues arise when considering the safety implications of wiring dwellings in poorer sections of communities and villages:

- In many countries, households with traditional thatched roof houses are not allowed an electricity supply because they do not have a permanent watertight roof. Thatched roofs for domestic dwellings are generally kept watertight, however, and, for extra safety, cable and fittings for exterior use can be specified. The dangers associated with running the service connection under the thatch can be prevented by specifying that either armoured cable or conduit is used up to the meter or load limiter.

○ Extensions to house wiring are often carried out by unqualified people in an attempt to save money. Wiring harnesses, as described above, can reduce the problem of dangerous wiring extensions by allowing households to re-position electrical fittings and add extra fittings with relative ease. Wiring harnesses are not as safe as properly installed fixed wiring, but are usually safer than the wiring found in the houses of poorer people. When used alone, they are appropriate for households that need only one or two light bulbs and perhaps a radio.

○ When more appliances are used, particularly those that must be earthed, the risk of electric shock increases and compulsory earth leakage protection should be considered. For high-current appliances, a meter is usually in-stalled and overcurrent protection is required because the meter itself does not protect the house wiring.

○ Electrical safety will be further improved by greater education on the dan-gers of electricity, and more inspections of house wiring.

○ When weighing up the safety requirements for electricity installation it is important to be aware of the safety implications of using kerosene and candles. These are often taken for granted because they are familiar.

○ Safety experts in electricity utilities and health and safety bodies should be consulted and options such as wiring harnesses and earth leakage circuit-breakers discussed. This information should be used to revise safety and electrical installation standards.

Credit

The provision of credit for the start-up costs of an energy supply scheme is a very positive incentive for rural energy supply. Households that may be unable to raise a large lump sum to cover the cost of a PV system, a share in a biogas scheme, or electricity connection and wiring costs, are often able to pay the same amount in instalments over a period of time, sometimes in part from savings on other fuels.

Credit for electricity installation and renewable energy equipment (such as PV) is available in quite a number of countries. The amount of credit available and the repayment period vary widely between countries. In some countries, for instance, an electricity system connection fee can be paid over a period of up to four or six months, whereas in Colombia, credit for a similar connection is available over two to four years. In a few cases, such as Sri Lanka and the Kutir Jyothi schemes in India, credit also covers house wiring. Credit may be best supplied by an external organization or by local electricity contractors, as util-ities often have their own cash flow problems and will be reluctant or unable to provide credit to consumers.

Tariff reforms

Tariffs should be set to give the energy scheme owner sufficient income to be financially viable, without discouraging consumers from either obtaining a supply or using the energy or electricity. The World Bank recommends a minimum tariff level of 8.5 cents per kilowatt hour in order to cover operating costs, make

Credit schemes are used worldwide to finance photovoltaic electricity supply systems

equity contributions to investment needs and attract loan financing on commercial terms. Tariffs are often set too low and result in the utilities running up large debts and being unable to maintain, let alone expand, the supply system.

Tariffs often consist of a fixed charge, or standing charge, and an energy charge. The fixed charge generally covers the cost of revenue collection. This can be reduced by using both load limiters and community involvement, as described in previous sections. Low-income households cannot afford to pay high fixed charges, as they have only a small amount of money with which to pay their complete electricity bill.

High energy costs are less of a deterrent than a high fixed charge. They are likely to restrict the amount of electricity consumed but are unlikely to deter low-income households from obtaining a supply. Some utilities provide a low tariff, often known as the 'lifeline tariff', for low-income households. This encourages low-income households to obtain a connection and helps them to pay for the electricity. However, the lifeline tariff should be restricted to very low consumption levels to prevent the utility being overburdened.

Government-controlled setting of tariff levels can greatly affect the development of sustainable energy supply schemes. For instance, where there are favourable electricity tariffs for grid electricity in rural areas (e.g. in India), tariff levels set to ensure payback on loans at the inception of privately owned or community-owned schemes may not be acceptable to users. There are cases in which users have decided that they would wait for the arrival of the grid line

34

(which can be several years away) rather than own and manage their own scheme for this reason.

Community ownership

The ownership of electrical or other energy supply systems does not have to be limited to energy companies. The option for rural communities to own their own supply system has many advantages, if they are prepared to undertake it. The suitability of this option will depend on local social and economic factors. Such ownership may be suitable where there is a history of community planned and owned development activities, or where local NGOs are able to facilitate participative planning of the supply. In fact, participation is important for the success of all privately owned schemes.

Community ownership will involve the establishment of a company, which may in the early stages have less than the majority of the equity owned by the community, but with successful profitable operation this ownership can be increased to 100 per cent over time. Successful management of the company will involve substantial training, and this is an important role for the public sector. In fact, the promotion of community ownership may be delegated by government to not-for-profit agencies, such as the rural electrification co-operatives which have been successful in various countries such as the Philippines or in parts of Latin America.

Community involvement can be very useful in the planning and installation of an electrification project and, in some cases, for tariff collection. The community can decide what it wants and how much it is prepared to contribute. Utilities can benefit from reduced costs, greater coverage, and ease of implementation.

Communities can also make contributions 'in kind' to the cost of providing an electricity supply, which may result in significant cost savings. Even if there is no tangible contribution of materials or labour, a good relationship between the utility and the community can lead to a greater sense of responsibility. The benefits of this are reduced theft and vandalism. In addition, social pressure can prevent individuals from obstructing the utility and/or making large claims for compensation for poor supply and service.

The community can lobby for a supply and encourage electrification by committing themselves to taking a given number of connections. They can facilitate planning by advising on the routing of the distribution lines and by assisting with any right-of-way disputes. They can elect a committee to aid communication between the utility and the community.

One disadvantage of community involvement is that, because local people become familiar with domestic electricity installation, they may be more likely to bypass load limiters and meters or make illegal connections. With metered consumers there are more problems with entrusting the community to provide a full revenue collection service. Households are more likely to default on payments as they may be faced with unexpectedly high bills that they cannot afford or refuse to pay because they consider that the revenue collector is overcharging them. The job of the revenue collector(s) is much more complicated as they must read the meters, keep accounts, and deal with more problems of defaults on payments. It is easier for the revenue collectors to overcharge the consumers or underpay the electricity company as the payments are not fixed, and therefore the company must carefully monitor the work of the revenue collectors and the energy supplied to the community. An alternative with metered consumers is for the job to be shared between the utility and the community, with the utility reading the meters and issuing the bills, and the community collecting the payments.

Community involvement is more likely in rural areas than in urban areas because communities are more cohesive and because cost savings have more impact as the economy is less cash based. In urban areas the use of local labour may also be a way of reducing installation costs.

Mobilizing community resources must be part of a deliberate coherent policy from the beginning. This has been true of the rural electrification programme in Thailand and the Andhi Khola project in Nepal. If these approaches are to be replicated successfully elsewhere, they must be carried out sensitively and carefully. Local community support cannot be taken for granted. Within rural communities there is often great inequality and exploitation. Organizations with rural development experience should be involved to ensure fairness in the design of the scheme. Even with such involvement, however, establishing community involvement can be a long and time-consuming process.

Private versus public sector

The debate about the role of the public sector versus that of the private sector is complex. It is not so much a conflict between advocates of total state control of energy supply on the one hand, and a totally private sector approach on the other, more a question of finding the right balance between the functions taken on by the state and by the private sector. The state can manage those aspects that the private sector will not take on, and provide the 'enabling environment' or the rules of the game under which the private sector will complement the role of the state.

Utility ownership
Electrical utility companies have traditionally been publicly owned in most countries in Africa, South Asia and Latin America. They have also had responsibility for providing electricity generation, transmission and distribution within the one company, often with monopoly rights for the supply of electricity. This system may have worked well in the early stages of electrification, with centralized planning, and governments financing the expansion of the system. The question may be posed, 'Does it continue to work well in a situation where government or donor funds are limited, and demand is growing faster than supply?' This situation often arises because of population growth, increasing incomes and industrialization. In such cases it has often been found that publicly owned companies have difficulty in managing expansion. Publicly owned utilities have also generally not been very successful at providing decentralized energy services in remote areas. The questions then arise:

o What should be the limits of responsibility of public utilities, and in what circumstances can the private sector do a better job?
o Will a private monopoly of local electricity supplies lead to poor service to the consumer?
o How should the private sector be regulated?
o What is the role of government in planning and setting standards?

The situation of public monopoly has been modified in many instances recently to allow private generation to supply the grid, or private local distribution. This has the effect of allowing local private development of smaller schemes, with public development of larger schemes. This can help to overcome the constraints of the management capacity of public utilities, and enable the growth of the generating capacity through a multiplicity of small schemes to ease the delay in the development of the large schemes. The contracts for private electricity generation have to be managed carefully, however, to ensure that the consumer and the main utility are treated fairly.

Privatization of utility companies is being undertaken in many countries, but in different forms. For example:

o the companies can be split regionally, while retaining 'vertical integration', i.e. generation, transmission and distribution, or
o the utility companies are 'un-bundled' so that private (and perhaps some public) generation companies can supply a centrally owned transmission system, and distribution can be owned by a separate company.

In the second case, the advantages of splitting the electricity supply industry in this way are generally greater for much larger utilities than for those that currently exist in smaller countries in Africa, Asia and Latin America, as the opportunities for creating competition in smaller grid systems are much less.

Access to electricity
It is now conventional wisdom that utility companies should concentrate on extending the electricity grid to areas of high population density and to larger industries. In areas of low population and low potential demand, the income from sales of electricity may well not cover the costs of extending transmission and distribution to consumers. In these cases, which may cover extensive rural areas, then decentralized generation and distribution of electricity will be more cost effective. The role of the public sector is then less clear. Utility companies are sometimes given an obligation to take on the role of providing electricity in these situations, but often this has to be heavily subsidized and can often be done much more rapidly and cost-effectively by involving the private sector. In fact, a third player comes into the picture: the rural community, which may ultimately be the owner of the energy supply systems offered by the private sector. Of course, even in the case of grid extension, as with decentralized electrification, the contractual and technical work can be undertaken by private contractors specializing in electrification.

The enabling environment

The government's role in providing an enabling environment, regulation of the industry, setting targets and promoting programmes of decentralized rural electrification, at a regional or national level, can be important. This may involve:

o developing a planning framework defining areas for grid extension and for decentralized electrification
o providing enabling legislation to allow the generation and sale of electricity by private parties
o defining priorities for regions or villages and targets for expansion of supply to new areas
o defining standard levels of service (which may be less than full availability in some cases)
o defining standard contract conditions and warranty requirements
o setting tariff levels, and a means of revising them over time
o providing technical and managerial training
o ensuring finance is available
o administering any subsidies for connection to consumers with low demand, and
o accrediting of service providers and specific equipment.

These functions might be delegated by government to a parastatal or non-government organization. There will then be a framework in which the private and public sectors operate for the provision of energy supplies. The government may, for example, decide to allocate concessions for supplying electricity through a competitive bidding process, as has happened over the last few years in parts of Argentina. The companies awarded concessions are committed to the provision of agreed standards of energy services to a particular section of the population.

The type of companies to pre-qualify for such work include:

o those that have experience of operating public services such as water, telecommunications or electricity supplies
o manufacturers and suppliers of diesel generators and renewable energy equipment, and
o contractors with experience of installing diesel, hydro or other energy supply equipment.

The public sector is responsible for monitoring the compliance by the private sector service providers with energy/electricity services. This may involve instituting a quality management system which monitors consumer satisfaction. This approach involves considerable supervision and regulation by the public sector. It is likely to work best in countries where only a minority of the population does not already have a supply from the utility, and where the areas to be supplied under concession have strong local government.

The initial cost of connection is a barrier for poorer consumers in many cases. Utilities may provide some financial support for the initial connection costs, either through the provision of specific subsidies or through support for credit schemes. In South Africa, for instance, consumers in rural areas were given the option of paying for the connection themselves and then paying the normal tariff, or having a free connection and paying a higher tariff. The majority chose the higher tariff.

Finance may also be extended for working capital for equipment suppliers and for leasing equipment for household energy systems or for electrical connection costs. In the case of individual household energy devices, the government may also have a role in setting standards for private sector suppliers – for example, for solar home systems, solar lanterns, electrical safety, dam and weir safety and minimum river flows for hydroelectric plants.

Above all, the public sector may set targets for the extent of provision of electricity to its citizens, and can then institute various policies and market instruments to enable and stimulate the private sector to achieve these targets.

3

Assessing impact and success

Environmental impacts

In the past two decades environmental issues have become an ever-increasing global concern. Words such as 'sustainability', 'global warming' and 'biodiversity' are now commonly used. International concern was expressed recently at the United Nations Framework Convention on Climate Change, in Kyoto in 1997, where international conventions on global warming and biodiversity were signed by many world leaders. Environmental implications must now be considered in every new development. This chapter aims to explain the environmental issues relevant to rural energy planning and to describe methods for environmental assessment that will assist the planners when prioritizing projects in environmental terms.

Environmental impacts of energy systems

Environmental impacts are generally classified into three categories depending on the range over which the impact is felt:

○ local: impacts in a very localized area within a country, for example, household smoke pollution
○ regional: affecting more than one country or state, with cross-border implications, for example deforestation
○ global: affecting all parts of the world equally, with international implications, for example global warming

Impact Range of Environmental Problems

	Local	Regional	Global
Global warming			✓✓✓
Fossil fuel depletion		✓✓	✓✓✓
Ecological health	✓✓✓	✓✓	✓
Deforestation	✓✓✓	✓✓	✓✓
Toxic emissions (Environmental health)	✓✓✓	✓	

(✓✓✓ very significant impact, ✓✓ significant impact, ✓ some impact)

There may be other very specific environmental concerns, such as noise from a wind turbine, the smell from a biodigester or the visual impact of an unsightly power plant. These are generally associated with local planning laws rather than environmental assessment, and so will not be discussed here.

Global warming

This is the effect that a group of emissions, called greenhouse gases, are believed to have on the global climate. When these gases are present they allow the solar radiation to enter the atmosphere, but do not allow reflected heat to escape. There is therefore a gradual increase in the global temperature. Although it is generally agreed that there is a greenhouse effect occurring, there has been some dispute about the magnitude of the problem. Many scientists, including those from the International Panel on Climate Change (IPCC), have been considering what would happen if there was a significant change in climate over the next century, which could possibly melt the polar caps, causing the sea levels to rise, and extend the spread of deserts.

Ecological health and biodiversity

The ecological system, or natural environment, sustains a huge range of natural systems that are vital for the maintenance of life on earth. Any energy system that impacts on the local eco-system will have potential to impact on the ecological health of the local area. Biofuels have the greatest potential for damaging the ecosystem, unless the fuel supply is from a sustainable forestry resource. Also, if natural growth is cleared for land to cultivate a biofuel crop, then natural resources and biodiversity may be lost. Other energy sources, which build over natural landscapes or interact with the natural system, may affect the local ecology. An assessment of potential ecological damage must be made before any new development, to ensure particularly that endangered species are not damaged or that an essential local natural resource is not lost.

Deforestation

The felling of forests (tropical and temperate) without re-planting new trees will result in deforestation. This has particular implications for biodiversity, as forests sustain not just trees, but many other varieties of plants and many species of animals. Loss of forests will mean loss of natural habitats for plants and animals.

The main reasons for deforestation lie with commercial logging, or forest clearance for building or agriculture rather than for fuel.

This slope in Nepal has lost most of its forest cover

Photograph: Intermediate Technology

Although wood as fuel is not the main reason for deforestation, the impact of deforestation will be felt by people collecting wood for cooking and heating. The increasing use of wood for charcoal or fuelwood to be sold in urban areas is becoming a threat to forests.

Deforestation has knock-on effects on soil degradation and erosion. During a study in Ethiopia, it was found that where tree cover had been lost the mechanisms for returning nutrients to the topsoil were greatly reduced. This was due both to the loss of trees and to the use of agricultural waste for fuel instead of fertilizer.

Toxic emissions (environmental health)
Environmental health will impact in two ways. In urban areas, the combined toxic emissions from a number of sources (cars, industry, domestic fuel) increase the concentration of toxins in the ambient air to the point where it affects the health of the people in the local area. More common in rural areas, as well as in poorer urban houses, is indoor air pollution. Biomass cooking stoves emit smoke into the cooking area.

Smoke contains toxic emissions, including particulates and carbon monoxide (CO), which impact directly on the health of the cook and younger children who spend time in the kitchen with their mother. The main illnesses associated with indoor air pollution are acute respiratory infection (ARI) in the form of pneumonia, cancer, and adverse impacts on pregnancy. About one-third of deaths in children under five in developing countries are as a result of ARI and pneumonia. In addition, breathing problems and eye irritations are an everyday result of smoke pollution. Improved cooking stoves will help to reduce the problem of smoke, although there will have to be consideration of smoke extraction from households before the problem is eradicated completely.

Cooking stoves emit smoke into living areas

Photograph: Intermediate Technology

Environmental controls
There are a number of mechanisms that control environmental impacts. The mechanism will usually depend on the geographical scale of the environmental impact. Control mechanisms include:

42

International conventions and targets
(e.g. international conventions on global warming and biodiversity at Rio and Kyoto) take the form of a formal agreement by world leaders to aim for environmental goals. The main means of enforcement is through international political pressure to abide by the convention.

Regional agreements
(e.g. regional agreements on water rights or protection agreements on species of plants and animals) are mutual agreements between two or more countries with the aim of tackling a cross-boundary environmental problem. The individual countries involved in the agreement will usually regulate these.

National regulations and laws
(e.g. emission standards for combustion plants or waste liquid emissions to water courses) are set in place to regulate national environmental problems. The most common regulations are in the form of emissions standards for various types of industry, including fuel combustion plants for industry and power production. These are usually controlled through prosecution and fines for infringement of the regulation.

Local regulations
(e.g. regulations on tree felling) will be very specific regulations for the local area, which will aim to protect a locally sensitive ecosystem. They can be used to govern issues such as access to water and fuel, and can take the form of traditional rights (such as family water rights) or more modern developments such as rules set out by water committees or community forestry management teams.

Assessment of the environmental impacts of rural energy systems
Two approaches for assessing the impact of development projects are briefly described below.

Environmental impact assessment
An environmental impact assessment (EIA) is a study of the impact of a development on the local area, in terms of impacts on the natural ecosystem (land, water and air pollution), the health impacts on the local population, and the disturbance to the surroundings (visual, noise, smell, traffic congestion). There may be an estimate of potential accidental or sudden environmental impacts (for example, sudden large gas emissions).

There are three basic stages to the EIA:

○ a site-specific scoping and baseline survey
○ the prediction and evaluation of impacts, and
○ the preparation of environmental impact statement.

The first step is about understanding the existing situation, into which the development will take place. This is the assessment of the environmental characteristics of the area without the development. It is essential to record this situation so that future impacts can be compared to initial conditions. The second stage involves the prediction of potential environmental problems and an evaluation of the impact they will have on the local area. The prediction is the quantitative description of possible impacts of the study, and evaluation is a judgement of the importance of these impacts. Often the impacts are determined in terms of risk assessment, which must take into account the probability that the event will occur and also the impact that the event will have if it does occur. The final stage is the preparation of an environmental impact statement, which describes the predicted impact of the development.

The environmental impact statement will be the basis on which a decision is made as to whether a development will go ahead as it is proposed, or whether changes have to be made to ensure the environmental impact is minimized. Also, if more than one development project is proposed, the impact assessments for the projects can be compared to choose the project with least impact.

Fuel cycle assessment
Whereas an EIA makes a detailed assessment of the location where an energy project is established, a fuel cycle assessment (FCA) evaluates the environmental impact of the whole chain of processes involved in producing the useful energy.

This will include the impacts of:

○ extracting or collecting the fuel from the earth
○ manufacturing the energy conversion equipment
○ transporting equipment and fuel
○ the fuel combustion or energy conversion process, and
○ disposing of any wastes from the processes.

Once the full fuel cycle is determined, the following stages take place:

○ *Inventory* of all emissions from and resources used over the fuel cycle
○ *Impact assessment* of the potential environmental problems from the fuel cycle
○ *Evaluation* of the importance of these impacts

The assessment may consider all possible impacts of the cycle, including greenhouse gases, toxic emissions, resource depletion and so on. It is also possible to do a limited study of one or two aspects, depending on the main aims of the assessment. For example, it is sometimes useful to look at the primary energy inputs of the fuel cycle (in terms of fossil fuel inputs) to compare these with the energy outputs over the life of the energy project. This is sometimes termed 'energy accounting'.

By assessing the full fuel cycle, the full implications of a new energy development are determined. For example, where a diesel generator will have high emissions during the diesel generator operation, a solar cell will have low environmental impacts during use, but the solar cell manufacturing process uses a number of toxic chemicals and has a high energy input.

The FCA will determine which aspect of the fuel cycle has the greatest environmental impacts. This method may help to determine where investment in improved technologies will result in the greatest environmental improvement. For example, would it be more environmentally beneficial to invest in improving the efficiency of charcoal stoves, or in improving the efficiency of producing charcoal itself?

There may be some conflicting outcomes of an FCA. For example, where wood fuel is scarce it may seem sensible to substitute kerosene for wood for cooking. However, in global terms, wood is a renewable resource but kerosene use depletes fossil fuel reserves. The decision between local impacts over global impacts is often a political issue.

Factors affecting scheme success

Many energy supply schemes have been implemented in rural communities: some have succeeded, some have failed. What are the reasons for this? How, in fact, do we assess how successful a scheme is at delivering energy service requirements to a rural community?

This section rounds off the first part of the book. It draws together all the 'software' issues discussed in Part I, and examines the way in which they can interact as a whole. Issues that can have an impact on scheme success are:

○ the decision-making process and management
○ the way in which energy service needs are assessed
○ ability to pay and tariff levels
○ competition and reliability
○ relationships with equipment suppliers, and
○ appropriate financing options.

Some of these are described in this section – for more details, see the other chapters in this book.

The decision-making process and management

The adoption of participatory approaches involving communities in the whole process (i.e. planning, installation, implementation, monitoring and the operation and maintenance of the scheme) has proved to have positive effects with respect to community self-confidence and empowerment, as illustrated by the following case study from Sri Lanka.

A participatory approach: Electricity Consumer Society (ECS) in Sri Lanka

Each community, to manage the planning, implementation, operation and maintenance of a decentralized micro-hydro plant, forms an ECS. Each household connected to the scheme belongs to the ECS, which is governed by a constitution prepared by the members. Each ECS member household pays a small membership fee (Rs.2 to Rs.5) plus a monthly tariff for electricity consumed.

The ECS is managed by a democratically elected committee comprising chairperson, secretary, treasurer, vice-chairperson, assistant secretary, assistant treasurer and about six to eight committee members depending on the size of the village. The executive committee of the ECS generally meets once a fortnight, and a general meeting is held once a month. The annual general meeting elects the executive committee of the ECS.

Despite the emphasis put on participatory approaches and the community's involvement to ensure the success of a scheme, in many instances schemes are being implemented without any real participation of the beneficiaries. As a result, a scheme may be poorly designed and often the management of the scheme, which is crucial, is largely neglected. Such a situation can create social and economic conflicts when the project is completed. For example, when poor beneficiaries are excluded from the management of a scheme, decisions on tariffs and allocation of power may be made in a discriminatory way.

Needs assessment

When needs are not properly assessed – taking into account social and cultural dimensions as well as the different categories of end-uses (domestic, productive and social services) – the project is either over- or under-sized. For example, over-sizing a micro-hydro scheme means that

- more water is needed: i.e. a larger canal and increase in civil work costs, or;
- higher head: i.e. larger (and more expensive) penstocks, and;
- larger machines: i.e. larger turbine, generator.

As a result there is a substantial increase in costs, and no way of changing the situation afterwards.

Turbine at Nyafaru micro-hydro scheme
Photograph: Intermediate Technology/Alison Doig

When the project is over-sized, the costs increase dramatically, particularly in the case of micro-hydro, where it is difficult to correct such mistakes.

Apart from the equipment, the rise in the cost is due to the transport, which is relatively high given the large quantities of material involved in the implementation of micro-hydro schemes.

In the case of under-sizing, the development of new end uses is compromised, particularly for productive activities such as grain milling, oil processing and battery charging. In addition, conflicts may arise between domestic needs and income-generating activities. This type of situation often leads to social frustration caused, for instance, by the inability to connect new households and to a loss of income due to the inability to supply power for productive end uses. For example, in Nyafaru micro-hydro

46

Tariffs, power allocation and beneficiaries: Micro-hydro in Zimbabwe

Tariffs for the Nyafaru scheme were set according to the number of amps allocated to each household. This method is derived from the practices of the utility (Zimbabwe Electricity Supply Authority: ZESA). In the Nyafaru scheme, the allocation of power varies between 1.1kW and 3.3kW. This is quite a high allocation in comparison with the experience of other countries (such as Nepal and Sri Lanka) with similar micro-hydro projects, where the allocation of power for domestic end uses does not usually exceed 500W.

In Nyafaru, the combination of the flat rate tariff and the importance assigned by users to the amount of power allocated has led households to connect as many appliances as they can. This practice is possible because the scheme uses no monitoring or load-limiting devices (such as circuit breakers). Most countries that use flat rate tariff schemes use load limiters, so this is unusual. In addition, the fact that about one-third of the households are not connected gives consumers the impression that some capacity is still available. Some households use very large loads such as electric hotplates, and the utilization of a heater (which takes an enormous amount of power) has been recorded in one case. The use of such devices has, of course, led to overloading of the supply system, which is likely to reduce the life expectancy of the electro-mechanical equipment considerably.

Adapted from: Fernando, S., Khennas S., Rai K.: 'Evaluation of Nyafaru micro hydro plant', February 1997, ITDG report.

scheme in Zimbabwe, power was allocated in a way that favoured higher-income households.

Ability to pay and tariff levels

In the case of stand-alone systems, unlike centralized schemes, the beneficiaries alone must meet the cost of operation and maintenance. This means that even when the schemes are partially or entirely subsidized, the management committee must find a simple model in order to set up the tariffs, to collect the fees and to manage the scheme. When the tariffs are set at a level that is below the costs of operation and maintenance, including the labour of the operators, the community will be confronted by either an increase in tariffs or the prospect of the scheme closing down.

Consumers often have the means to pay higher tariffs from the outset, but are very reluctant to accept a dramatic increase in the tariffs afterwards. In order to determine the level the customers are willing to support, a golden rule is :

Assess the expenses the customers are used to paying (e.g costs of candles, hurricane lamps, batteries) *before* the introduction of the scheme.

The community's contribution should cover at least all the running costs, which include:

○ salaries of operators (part time or full time)
○ payment of interest and capital when a loan has been taken out

47

○ spare parts, and
○ fuel cost, if any.

If schemes must make loan repayments at commercial rates, the planning process must also take into account these costs. For some renewable energies, such as photovoltaics, the supplier can repossess the equipment if the community or the beneficiary fails to complete the repayment. In other cases, interest-free credit is granted for a short period of time (three to six months). If the customer fails to complete the repayment, he or she then has to repay the loan plus interest.

Example of a household photovoltaic (PV) system in Kenya
System cost: US$500
Down payment: 50 per cent plus 25 per cent on installation
Repayment period: remaining 25 per cent within three months
Interest rate: 0 per cent if repayment complete within agreed period, 15 per cent if payment is not complete after agreed period. Repossession is a possible option.

When it appears that the running costs exceed the previous energy expenses, consultation with the users is crucial to find out if the community is willing to support higher energy expenses in order to benefit from a better quality of service. Apart from the running costs, a fund to connect other customers and/or develop new productive end uses is important to the sustainability of the scheme.

Competition and reliability

When a new scheme such as a micro-hydro power plant is implemented, customers expect a better quality of service compared with existing facilities, if any, or with traditional methods and equipment.

In the case of grain milling, the distance to the facility, processing time, the quality of the product, the rates and scheme reliability are important factors to attract customers and to disseminate the innovations in the area.

Experiences in many countries show that people revert to traditional methods or diesel equipment when new systems break down or fail to deliver the expected results. After this, it is very difficult to reverse the process and to rebuild customer confidence.

Relationships with equipment suppliers

So far, there is no established tradition in dealing with suppliers. Some schemes are commissioned without following suppliers' instructions and guidelines. When the owners are not responsible for implementing the scheme (which is common practice), they are not aware of all the clauses in the contract and the possible guarantees attached to the equipment. For example, a ten-year guarantee is generally given with solar PV panels.

Although the margin of negotiation is narrow with established equipment suppliers in some countries, some options are available in order to include clauses on the guarantee of equipment life expectancy and after-sales service. Experience gathered all over the world for various forms of renewable energy shows that this parameter is crucial in the sustainability of small schemes.

Appropriate financing options
Experience has also shown that appropriate financing packages can support the development of rural energy schemes. In many cases, finding the initial capital for investment is the greatest barrier to scheme installation, and several approaches now exist to overcome this (see the section on Financing options in Chapter 2). It is also true that inappropriate financing options can have a severe impact on rural communities, to the extent that they not only end up without an energy supply scheme, but are also in the position of having put themselves into a level of debt from which they will struggle to liberate themselves.

Assessing success
One of the most difficult things about an energy scheme is to assess its level of success after it has been operating for a few years. It is also difficult to know when is the best time to make this assessment. Consider an example in which the scheme performs well for the first few years because the original team that installed the scheme can provide support. After four or five years, the scheme could suffer and begin to have problems, while the managers work out how to keep it going in the long term.

Eventually the scheme could settle down and become relatively free of problems. Here the scheme will seem like a success if assessed initially; will seem to be more of a failure if assessed in the middle period; and then will appear as a success again if assessed as the scheme settles down. It is difficult to say what period is best for the assessment of schemes, but in general, it should be possible to assess scheme performance within two or three years of commissioning, and to take into account the performance of the scheme over the previous years when doing so.

In order to do this, it is best to return to the original assessment of energy needs made when designing the scheme in the first place and to use this as a measure of how well the scheme has done in meeting them. (See the section in Chapter 1 on Energy service requirements, and particularly the Energy service survey guide (the checklists). In assessing scheme performance, it is important to divide the community in the same way as when originally assessing energy needs.

PART II

TECHNICAL OPTIONS

4

Conventional technologies

Diesel

The internal combustion (IC) engine has been used for many decades and plays a very important role in providing power for rural applications. Many stand-alone units provide power for milling, small-scale electricity production, water pumping, etc. They are readily available commercially off-the-shelf in most major towns and cities in developing countries, in a range of sizes for various applications. There is usually a well established spare parts and maintenance network, at both urban and rural centres.

Diesel-driven pump
Photograph: Intermediate Technology

There are two main types of IC engine, and they can be simply categorized by the type of fuel used; petrol (gasoline) or diesel. The petrol engine is widely used for small vehicles and light applications, whereas diesel engines are more suited to continuous running for lengthy periods at higher load ratings and are therefore used more widely for stationary applications and commercial vehicles.

Technical

Principles of operation of the IC engine

As mentioned above, the main distinction in common engine types is that of the fuel used. The combustion process in the petrol engine and the diesel engine differ in the following significant features: in the petrol engine the petrol and air mixture is drawn into the cylinder, compressed (compression ratios ranging from 4:1 to 10:1), and ignited by a spark introduced by an electrical system. In the diesel engine, on the other hand, air alone is drawn into the cylinder and is compressed to a much higher ratio (14:1 to 25:1) than in the petrol engine. As a result of this compression, the air is heated to a temperature of 700–900°C. Only then is a certain quantity of diesel

53

fuel injected into the cylinder and, because of the prevailing high temperature, the fuel ignites spontaneously. Hence the petrol engine is often referred to as the spark ignition (SI) engine and the diesel as the compression ignition (CI) engine.

There is also the sub-division according to cycle type: the two-stroke or four-stroke cycle. This categorization differentiates between engines that have an ignition phase on every revolution of the crankshaft, or every other revolution. The method of mixing and injecting air and fuel is different for the two cycle types. The bulk of IC engines use the four-stroke cycle, based on the cycle first proposed by Alphonse Beau de Rochas in 1862 and later developed by Nikolaus Otto (petrol) and Rudolph Diesel (diesel). Here we shall look at the principle of operation of the four-stroke engine.

Since power is developed during only one stroke, the single cylinder four-stroke engine develops a pulsating torque and output power. Smoother running is obtained either with a flywheel, or with a combination of a flywheel and multi-cranks that are staggered in relation to one another on the crankshaft. There are many variations of engine configuration, e.g. 4 or 6 cylinder, in line, horizontally opposed, vee or radial configurations

Table 4.1 shows a comparison of the relative practical advantages and disadvantages of petrol and diesel engines.

Table 4.1: Advantages and disadvantages of petrol versus diesel engines

Diesel	Petrol
Pros	*Pros*
Lower fuel costs	Light – hence more portable
Higher efficiencies	Lower capital costs
Readily available for a wide range of sizes and applications	Cheaper to maintain
Lower running speeds	Higher running speeds
Cons	*Cons*
Maintenance is more expensive	Not so durable – especially under continuous long-term usage
Heavier and bulkier for a given power	Lower efficiency for equivalent power
Higher capital cost	Fuel more expensive
Pollution	Narrower range of off-the-shelf engines available – smaller engines more readily available
	Pollution

Application and choice of engine

To make a decision as to the type of engine that is most suitable for a specific application, several factors need to be considered. The two most important are the power and the speed of the engine. The power requirement is determined by the maximum load. The engine power rating should be 10–20 per cent more than the power demand imposed by the end use. This prevents overloading the machine by inadvertently adding extra load during the starting of motors, or with some types of lighting systems, or as wear and tear on the machinery pushes up its power consumption.

For example, a generator with a required output of 10 kilowatts and an efficiency of 75 per cent would require an engine of the following capacity:

Output requirement	10kW
Efficiency	0.75
Shaft power requirement	$10/0.75 = 13.3kW$
Engine power requirement	$13.3kW \times 110\% = 14.63kW$

Since engine power is usually given in horsepower (1 hp = 0.746kW), we should choose an engine of size 19.6 hp or the next standard size *above* this figure.

Another important factor when choosing an engine is its speed. Speed is measured at the output shaft and is given in revolutions per minute (r.p.m.). An engine will operate over a range of speeds, with diesel engines typically running at lower speeds (1300–3000 r.p.m.) and petrol engines at higher speeds (1500–5000 r.p.m.). There will be an optimum speed at which fuel efficiency will be greatest. Engines should be run as close as possible to their rated speed to avoid poor efficiency and the build up of engine deposits due to incomplete combustion, which will lead to higher maintenance and running costs. To determine the speed requirement of an engine we again look at the requirement of the load. For some applications, the speed of the engine is not critical but for other applications – a generator for example – it is important to get a good speed match. If a good match can be obtained then direct coupling is possible; if not, then some form of gearing will be necessary – a gearbox or belt system for example, which will add to the overall cost and reduce the efficiency.

There are various other factors that have to be considered when choosing an engine for a given application. These include the following: cooling system, abnormal environmental conditions (dust, dirt, etc.), fuel quality, speed governing (fixed or variable speed), poor maintenance, control system, starting equipment, drive type, ambient temperature, altitude and humidity. Suppliers' or manufacturers' literature will provide the required information when purchasing an engine.

Uses and power requirements
As mentioned earlier, there is wide range of applications for the diesel or petrol engine. Some typical rural applications and their power requirements are shown below:

Application	Typical power requirement
Small-scale irrigation pumps	2–15kW
Small-scale electricity generation	2–50kW
Battery charging	500W
Grain milling or threshing	5–15kW

Diesel generator sets are used throughout the world

Photograph: Intermediate Technology/Neil Cooper

Diesel generator sets

Because of their widespread use throughout the world, diesel generator sets deserve a further mention. Diesel generating sets come in a wide range of commercially available sizes, from about 5kW up to 30MW. They are long lasting and will usually have a useful lifespan of seven to ten years (30 000 hours running time), but this can be drastically reduced if maintenance is poor.

They are installed by individuals, electricity utilities and businesses, and are often used to supply a small electrical grid in remote areas that the national grid has not yet reached. They are usually fitted with a governor, which automatically controls the speed of the machine as the load varies, thus maintaining constant voltage and frequency.

Efficiency depends on the loading of the machine, and where the load pattern (the pattern of electricity consumption throughout the day) requires it, two or more smaller machines are used to achieve higher fuel efficiency. Diesel generator sets, being somewhat noisy, are usually sited in a separate powerhouse away from the premises, or outside the town (depending upon their application).

Petrol generator sets come in smaller sizes – from 500W up to several kW – and tend to have a much shorter lifespan (5000 hours running time) than their diesel counterparts. They are more suited to mobile, very small-scale electricity needs.

Alternative fuels

IC engines have been designed to operate on petroleum fuels; however, their operation is not confined to these fuels. Ethanol and methanol (also known as alcohols) substitute directly for petrol (gasoline), and vegetable oils can substitute directly for diesel fuels. Since the 1970s the threat of more expensive petroleum fuels has encouraged the examination of these and other alternatives produced from biomass. Ethanol is already used commercially as an engine fuel in Brazil and, when blended with petrol to form the blend known as gasohol, in a number of other countries. The availability of alternative fuels for IC engines means that for the foreseeable future IC engines are still serious contenders for stationary applications to provide shaft power, particularly at the lower end of the power range.

Issues

Hybrid systems

In some cases hybrid or mixed systems are used to provide a flexible and cost-effective alternative to pure diesel or pure petrol systems. These are systems that combine two or more technologies that enhance one another's capabilities. For example, a wind turbine can be used in conjunction with a diesel generating set. When the output from the wind turbine drops below a certain power level, due to lack of wind, the diesel generator can be switched in to compensate. These systems can be a combination of purely renewable energy technologies or combine fossil fuel energy technologies, depending on the circumstances. Careful planning is needed when considering such a system.

Cost

Cost plays an important role in the choice of technology for rural applications. There are two main costs to consider when contemplating different options – the investment cost and the running costs. For diesel systems, such as for irrigation pumps, for corn mills, or for electricity generators, the equipment costs are low compared with renewable energy technologies, but the running costs are higher. Running costs depend directly on the amount of energy used and on the cost of fuel. It is worth bearing in mind that, in the long term, the fuel costs for a diesel or petrol engine will be high compared with the capital cost. However, if a diesel engine is used for milling, for example, the extra cost of adding a generator to supply electricity for lighting or battery charging may be quite low. Many machines sit unused for long periods because of lack of funds for fuel or simply scarcity of imported fuel. Fuel can also easily be stolen. See the Cost comparison of energy options section in Chapter 6 for information and comparisons on costs of different power supply sources.

Suppliers, spare parts and maintenance

One important factor to consider when purchasing an engine is the availability of spare parts in the country. If there is within the country a dealership or supplier for the manufacturer of the machine that you will be buying, then there should be no problem obtaining spare parts. Indeed, many machines are now manufactured in developing countries. There is usually a wide range of manufacturers represented in major towns and cities in most countries throughout the world. It is worth checking this before purchase. Some countries are affected by embargoes or trade restrictions, which can make it difficult to find spares.

Maintenance of any machine in the developing world is a recurring theme that has been given a great deal of attention, but which still presents many problems. It is important to ensure that the machine will be maintained regularly by a competent person. In remote rural areas this can present problems. There is often no one in the area with knowledge of the machine – and letting unskilled people maintain the machine can be worse than doing nothing at all. It will be very expensive to bring in a skilled mechanic from the nearest town (which may be several days away) to carry out the maintenance. It is often worth considering sending a local person for training so that the maintenance will be carried out regularly and competently.

Kerosene and liquid petroleum gas

The vast majority of people in developing countries use biomass fuels for all their energy requirements. These include a wide range of fuels such as fuelwood, charcoal, crop residues and animal dung. In rural areas few other fuel sources are available or affordable. As people's incomes grow, however, they begin to use 'modern' fuels more extensively. When people can afford kerosene and gas (LPG) they prefer these fuels to fuelwood or dung for cooking. As can be seen from Figure 4.1, kerosene and LPG are many times more efficient, less damaging to the health and are much easier to use for cooking. Kerosene is also widely used for lighting in developing countries.

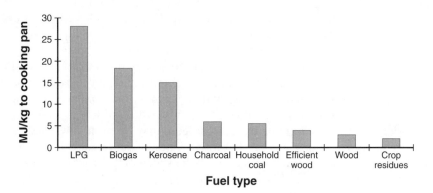

Figure 4.1: *Energy efficiency of selected cooking fuels*
Source: *Rural Energy and Development*, The World Bank, Washington DC, 1996

Technical

How kerosene and gas were formed, and are extracted and refined
Kerosene is a liquid fossil fuel. It is usually transported in bulk, and in rural areas of developing countries is usually purchased by the litre or bottle. It is commonly found in rural centres where it is sold by small retailing outlets or garages.

Kerosene is used mainly for cooking and lighting. An appropriately designed kerosene stove can be efficient and cook quickly. It is easily controlled, convenient and popular in comparison with other rural cooking technologies. Using kerosene can prevent illnesses related to a smoky environment, will help save trees, and cuts down the time required for fuelwood collection in areas where fuelwood is already scarce.

On the other hand, kerosene stoves give off an unpleasant smell and can be dangerous when handled improperly or when faulty equipment is used. Lighting

58

Kerosene is sold in rural centres throughout the world

Photograph: Intermediate Technology/Lindel Caine

a kerosene stove is also tedious, and they can be noisy when running. The cost of purchasing kerosene is prohibitive in many parts of the developing world and quality is often poor.

Liquid Petroleum Gas (LPG) or bottled gas comprises butane or propane, which are hydrocarbon gases produced during the petroleum refining process. They are gaseous at normal temperatures but when compressed become liquid. LPG is typically purchased in cylinders of various sizes. It is used predominantly for cooking and is very easy to use, is efficient and burns cleanly. The high initial cost of purchasing appliances and cylinders, the relatively sophisticated technology, irregularity of supply and risk of explosion mean that it is not widely used in the majority of poorer areas. Cylinders are usually exchanged at filling stations, and since there are few of these in rural areas and transport is poor, access to this fuel source is also difficult.

The hardware

Kerosene

There are various types of stoves and lamps available. There are two main types of stove – the wick stove and the pressurized stove. There is little to choose between the two. The pressure stove is more powerful but is also generally more expensive and more prone to accidents due to the complexity of the lighting technique and the pressurized contents. A brief description of each kind of stove is given below.

59

The wick stove. Wick stoves can have one or more wicks. Improved kerosene wick stoves can have up to 30 or 40 wicks and produce a maximum power of around 5kW with an efficiency of up to 50 per cent. A common design incorporates a series of wicks, usually made of loosely twisted or woven cotton, placed in a holder so that they can be moved up and down by a control lever or knob.

The pressure stove. The standard kerosene pressure stove comprises a fuel tank (often pressurized by means of a hand-operated plunger pump), a vapour burner and a pot holder. Vaporized kerosene fuel is passed under pressure through a nozzle and mixes with primary air to form a strong blue flame. To initiate the process, the vaporizer has to be preheated using an alcohol-based flame which burns for several minutes in a tray placed below the vaporizer. Once the temperature of the vaporizer has been raised sufficiently, the kerosene can then be vaporized by the heat of the cooking flame and the alcohol flame can be allowed to extinguish. The pressure forces kerosene through the vaporizer continuously and is controlled by the adjustment valve or by regulating the pressure of the tank, which in turn controls the flame intensity. Again, there are various designs based on the same operating principle, some with more than one vaporizer fitted to provide multiple cooking rings. Another means of pressurizing the kerosene is to use a header tank. This does away with the need for a pressurized tank but also makes the stove more cumbersome. Typical maximum power output is in the range of 3–10kW.

Kerosene pressure stove
Photograph: Intermediate Technology

To assess the technical performance of a kerosene stove, the following factors need to be considered:

○ maximum power
○ efficiency at different power outputs
○ ability to control power output – known as the turn-down ratio
○ safety standards

The turn-down ratio is important as food often has to be simmered at low power output.

Lighting. The options are similar when we look at kerosene lighting technology. The two main lamp types are the wick and pressure lamps. The pressure lamp, commonly known as the 'Tilley' or 'Petromax' lamp, works on the same principle as the pressurized stove but the flame emerges inside an incandescent mantle which provides visible light.

The wick lamp comes in various forms – from the simple, locally made, wick-in-a-can, to the more sophisticated storm (or hurricane) lantern.

Example of a wick lamp
Photograph: Intermediate
Technology/RV Veladochaga

Hurricane lamp
Photograph: Intermediate Technology/Dai Rees

The efficiency of such lamps tends to be very low. Figure 4.2 shows a comparison of the luminous efficacy of various types of flame-based lighting technology.

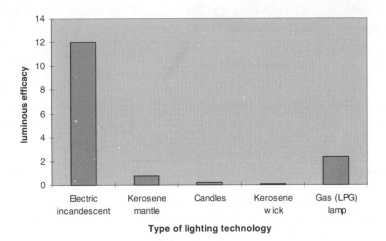

Figure 4.2: *Luminous efficacy of flame-based lighting*
Source: *Rural Energy and Development*, The World Bank, Washington DC, 1996
'Luminous efficacy' measures the amount of light emitted by a source divided by the amount of power consumed

LPG

LPG cooking stoves come in various shapes and sizes. They have a simple burning ring, pan support and use a 3 or 6kg LPG bottle. Multiple ring stoves with a combined oven are also available.

Use of LPG stove
Photograph: Intermediate Technology/M Lidbetter

Gas lamps use a rare earth incandescent mantle similar to the kerosene pressure lamp because otherwise the gas burns with a blue non-luminous flame. The lamps tend to be of simple construction, with the mantle holder and valve assembly fitted directly to the bottle.

Another application for LPG is refrigeration. The gas is used as a heating source in conjunction with an absorption refrigeration cycle to provide cooling for vaccines in hospitals – and cold drinks! Gas can also be used for sterilization processes in hospitals.

Other issues

Subsidies

Government subsidies are sometimes used to reduce the cost of a fuel to encourage its use, or to equalize the cost between different parts of the country. This is often the case in countries where there are shortages of traditional fuel sources or where the government feels a need to modernize the energy sector. These subsidies can often be counter-productive as they are expensive for the government, often consuming significant portions of the national budget, and limit the quantity of fuel available. Some argue that market liberalization is a more effective way of encouraging a change in fuel use habits.

Available alternatives – improved biomass stoves

An alternative to encouraging the use of 'modern' fuels is to provide low-cost methods of improving the efficiency and desirability of traditional fuel combustion technologies. Much work has been carried out throughout the developing world on improved stoves for use with biomass fuels. The main thrust of the work has been to improve efficiencies (to reduce fuel consumption and hence collection times) and to remove smoke from the user environment (to tackle the health problems associated with traditional fuel use). Many improved biomass stove techniques have been developed and adopted throughout the world. The availability and comparative cost of such stoves directly affects the need and the desire to change to modern fuel sources. (See the section on Biomass in Chapter 5).

Grid connection

Electricity is extremely versatile, clean, easy to use, and can be turned on or off at the flick of a switch. Electricity has brought enormous social benefits to all areas of life. It is the preferred method of supplying power for many household applications, especially lighting, but connection to the national electrical grid is a rare occurrence in rural areas of the developing world. In the majority of the worlds' poorer countries it is estimated that significantly less than 5 per cent of the rural population is connected to the national grid. There are many reasons, both technical and economic, that make grid connection unfeasible, and these will be looked at briefly in this section. In urban areas of the developing world, grid connection is commonplace.

There are other possibilities for providing electricity in rural areas. In many areas where electricity is required and there is no grid within easy reach then a localized grid (or micro-grid) can be established using a local power source, such as a diesel generator set or small-scale hydro power scheme. Alternatively, individual households can be connected to stand-alone systems which can be powered by any of a wide variety of energy sources.

Technical

The grid

The national grid is a network of power lines that allows transmission and distribution of electricity throughout all or part of a country. The grid can be connected to a single power source or electricity generating plant, but is usually linked with other plants to provide a more flexible and reliable network. The electricity is usually transmitted at very high voltage, typically several hundred thousand volts (depending on power transmitted, national guidelines, etc.) as this reduces losses and means that smaller conductors can be used, reducing the overall cost of the network. Bulk electricity is generated and transmitted in 3-phase alternating current (a.c. – 50 or 60Hz) and distributed to the consumer as 3-phase or single phase, depending on the end use requirements. Transmission by direct current (d.c.) is also used. Direct Current is used in preference to alternating current for long distance transmission because:

  ○ there is no requirement for a steady-state capacitative current
  ○ control is easier, and
  ○ it is easier to link systems operating at different frequencies.

The equipment needed to convert d.c. to and from a.c. is expensive and complex to operate, however, so d.c. is not always the best option.

After generation, the voltage is increased for transmission and distribution using a transformer and then reduced for end use, again requiring a transformer. The reduction process is usually done in several stages as the network is reduced in capacity. Typical domestic consumer voltage is 240V, depending on national standards.

Cost of grid connection
There are many constraints to rural grid-based electrification. Firstly there is the question of cost. Capital cost of the distribution system is very high and density of demand in rural areas is very low. Households can be widely dispersed and rural consumers will often want to use only a few light bulbs and a radio in the evening. There is little incentive for an electricity-producing utility to extend the grid into remote rural areas. Often, rural regional centres will be electrified but the network will usually stop there, or bypass the more remote villagers as high-voltage conductors passing overhead. In poorer communities the cost of house wiring, appliance purchase and electricity prices can also be prohibitive.

Grid system through a rural area
Photograph: Intermediate Technology/Steve Fisher

Other barriers to grid connection
Although the introduction of electricity to a community often stimulates income-generating activities and hence a gradual increase in the uptake of electricity use, the conditions for introducing electricity do not normally exist in rural areas. Most commercial and industrial activities are concentrated at the regional centres. In many developing countries the existing generating capacity is unable to cope with demand. Blackouts are a common occurrence in many major cities, especially as the process of rapid urbanization continues.

Low-cost grid connection
Where grid connection is an option, be it to the national grid or a micro-grid, then one method of making it affordable is to keep the connection costs and subsequent bills to a minimum. Often, rural domestic consumption is low. There are a number of solutions that can specifically help low-income households to obtain an electricity connection and help utilities meet their required return on investment. These include:

   ○ *Load limited supply*. Load limiters work by limiting to a prescribed value the current supplied to the consumer. If the current exceeds that value then

64

the device automatically disconnects the power supply. The consumer is charged a fixed monthly fee irrespective of the total amount of energy consumed. The device is simple and cheap, and does away with the need for an expensive meter and subsequent meter reading.

o *Reduced service connection costs.* Limiting load supply can also help reduce the costs of the conductor, as the maximum power drawn is low and so smaller conductor sizes can be used. Also, alternative cable poles can sometimes be found to help reduce costs.

o *Pre-fabricated wiring systems.* Wiring looms can be manufactured 'ready to install', which will not only reduce costs but also guarantee safety standards.

o *Credit.* Credit schemes can allow householders to overcome the barrier imposed by the initial entry costs of grid connection. Once connected, energy savings on other fuels can enable repayments to be made. Using electricity for lighting, for example, is a fraction of the cost of using kerosene.

o *Community involvement.* Formation of community committees and co-operatives who are proactive in all stages of the electrification process can help reduce costs as well as provide a better service. For example, community revenue collection can help reduce the cost of collection for the utility and hence the consumer.

Areas of application

Uses

There is wide range of applications for electricity. Electrical motors provide shaft power which can be used for a multitude of industrial and agricultural activities, as well as for transport. Batteries allow electricity to be stored for periods when it will be required. In a rural context, electricity has many uses. They include some of the following:

Domestic	Other
Lighting – probably the most important from the rural user's viewpoint	Irrigation pumps
Communication – tv, radio, etc.	Agro processing (including milling, oil extraction, threshing, etc.)
Water heating	Small workshops (carpentry, metal working, automotive, etc.)
Cooking	
Refrigeration	Hospitals and health centres
Sewing machines	Small businesses – traditional rural industries
Water pumping from rivers, boreholes (community level)	and many more

The social impact of introducing electricity to a region can be enormous. There are the benefits of improved social services, such as lighting at health centres, hospitals and schools and refrigeration of vaccines. There are other social gains such as street lighting, cinema and television, and community services such as milling of grain, sawmills or battery charging (often an alternative to grid connections).

The introduction of electricity can help to create productive employment in rural areas and there is a positive impact on economic as well as social growth.

Specific issues

Grid vs. stand-alone

One way of avoiding the prohibitive cost of distribution networks is to decentralize the power generating capacity and install local small-scale, low-voltage grids, otherwise known as micro-grids. This tends to be the main thrust of the work being carried out on rural electrification in some countries at the present time. Localized grid networks allow local renewable resources to be exploited. Energy sources such as small-scale hydro power, solar (photovoltaic), windpower and biogas are all being employed successfully in rural electrification projects in the developing world.

Planning and implementation

Planning for an electrification programme at national level is a complex task. There are many things to be considered: energy policy, generating capacity, priority regions and areas, network design, matching supply and demand, market identification, technology options, load management, pricing, funding, centralized or decentralized generation, fuel options and national development policy.

5

Renewable energy sources

Biomass

What is biomass?

The exploitation of energy from biomass has played a key role in the evolution of mankind. Until relatively recently it was the only form of energy that was usefully exploited by humans, and is still the main source of energy for more than half the world's population for domestic energy needs.

Traditionally the extraction of energy from biomass is split into three distinct categories:

○ *Solid biomass* – includes the use of trees, crop residues, animal and human waste (although not strictly a solid biomass source, it is often included in this category for the sake of convenience), household or industrial residues for direct combustion to provide heat. Often the solid biomass will undergo physical processing such as cutting, chipping or briquetting, but it retains its solid form.

○ *Biogas* – is obtained by anaerobically (in an air-free environment) digesting organic material to produce the combustible gas methane. Animal waste and municipal waste are common feedstocks for anaerobic digestion. In the UK, for instance, municipal waste is used to produce gas, which is then burned.

○ *Liquid biofuels* – are obtained by processing plants, seeds or fruits of different types (e.g. sugar cane, oil seeds or nuts) using various chemical or physical processes to produce a usable, combustible, liquid fuel. Pressing or fermentation are used to produce oils or ethanol from industrial or commercial residues such as bagasse (sugarcane residue remaining after the sugar is extracted) or from energy crops grown specifically for this purpose. Biofuels are often used in place of petroleum-derived liquid fuels.

In this section we shall consider only solid biomass and its associated technologies. The other biofuels are covered in the next section, Biogas and liquid biofuels.

Biomass use

More than two billion people use biomass for most of their household energy needs. It is used mainly for cooking, heating water and domestic space heating. Table 5.1 shows household energy consumption as a percentage of total biomass consumption in a number of selected countries in Africa. Biomass is also widely used for non-domestic applications.

Biomass is available in varying quantities throughout the world – from densely forested areas in the temperate and tropical regions of the world, to sparsely vegetated arid regions where collecting wood fuel for household needs is a time-consuming and arduous task.

Table 5.1: Household energy consumption as a percentage of total biomass consumption in a number of selected African countries

Country	Biomass energy consumption (% of total energy consumption)	Household energy consumption (% of total biomass energy)
Burundi	94	78.5
Ethiopia	86	97
Kenya	70	93
Somalia	87	92
Sudan	84	90
Uganda	95	78.6

Source: Karekezi and Ranja, 1997

In recent decades, with the threat of global deforestation, much attention has been given to the efficient use of biomass (as well as introducing alternative fuels) in areas where wood fuel is in particular shortage. Although domestic wood fuel users suffer greatly from the effects of deforestation, the main cause of deforestation is the clearing of land for agricultural use and for commercial timber or wood fuel use.

Improved cookstove in Kenya

Photograph: Intermediate Technology/Neil Cooper

Many programmes have been established during the last three decades aimed at developing and disseminating improved stove technologies to reduce the burden, primarily borne by women, of wood fuel collection as well as reducing the health risks associated with burning wood fuel. Technologies have also been introduced to help with the processing of biomass, either to improve efficiency or to allow for easy transportation.

Crop and industrial biomass residues are now widely used in many countries to provide centralized, medium and large-scale production of process heat for electricity production or other commercial end uses. There are several examples in Indonesia of timber-processing plants using wood waste-fired boilers to provide heat and electricity for their own needs, and occasionally for sale to other consumers. In Guyana in South America, sugar mills produce most of their process heat and electricity from bagasse, the cane residue from sugar processing. This is common in the sugar industry worldwide.

Technical

Biomass resources

As mentioned earlier, natural biomass resources vary in type and content, depending on geographical location. For convenience, we can split the world's biomass producing areas into three distinct geographical regions:

○ *Temperate regions* – produce wood, crop residues such as straw and vegetable leaves, and human and animal wastes. In Europe, short rotation coppicing (SRC) has become popular as a means of supplying wood fuel for energy production on a sustainable basis. Fast-growing wood species such as willow are cut every two to three years and the wood chipped to provide a boiler fuel. In countries where large quantities of municipal waste are generated, it is often processed to provide useful energy either from incineration or through recovery of methane gas from landfill sites.

○ *Arid and semi-arid regions* – produce very little excess vegetation for fuel. People living in these areas may be affected by desertification and can have difficulty finding sufficient wood fuel.

○ *Humid tropical regions* – produce abundant wood supplies, crop residues, animal and human waste, commercial, industrial and agro- and food-processing residues. Rice husks, cotton husks and groundnut shells are all widely used, particularly to provide process heat for power generation. Sugarcane bagasse is processed to provide ethanol as well as being burned directly and many plants, such as sunflower and oil-palm, are processed to provide oil for combustion.

Combustion efficiency

For solid biomass to be converted into useful heat energy, it has to undergo combustion. During combustion the following processes occur:

○ *Drying* – the heat from the flames dries out the fuel and the water leaves as steam. The drier fuel burns more efficiently.

○ *Pyrolysis* – when the temperature reaches between 200° and 350°C, volatile gases are released. These gases burn with a yellow flame. The process is self-sustaining as the heat from the burning gases releases further gases from the unburned fuel. Oxygen has to be provided to sustain this part of the combustion process. When all the gases have been burnt off, charcoal remains.

○ *Oxidation* – at about 800°C the charcoal oxidizes or burns. Again, oxygen is required. Both Pyrolysis and Oxidation produce heat.

The efficiency of combustion varies, depending on many factors including fuel, moisture content and type of fuel. The design of the stove or combustion system also affects the overall efficiency and Table 5.2 gives an indication of the efficiencies of some typical systems (including non-biomass systems for comparison).

Table 5.2: Efficiencies of some biomass energy conversion systems

Type of combustion technology	Percentage efficiency
Three-stone fire	10–15
Improved wood-burning stove	20–25
Charcoal stove with ceramic liner	30–35
Sophisticated charcoal-burning stove	up to 40
Kerosene pressure stove	53
LPG gas stove	57

Source: Adapted from Kristoferson and Bokalders, 1991

Technologies

Improved stoves

Much of the research and development work carried out on biomass technologies for rural areas of developing countries has been based on the improvement of traditional stoves. This was initially in response to the threat of deforestation, but has also been focused on the needs of women to reduce fuel collection times and improve the kitchen environment by smoke removal. There have been many approaches to stove improvement, some carried out locally and others as part of wider programmes run by international organizations. Figure 5.1 shows a variety of successful improved stove types, some small, portable stoves and others designed for permanent fixture in a household.

Improved stove design is a complex procedure which needs a broad understanding of many issues. Involvement of users in the design process is essential to gain a thorough understanding of the user's needs and requirements for the stove. The stove is not merely an appliance for heating food (as it has become in Western society), but is often acts as a social focus, and a means of lighting and space heating. Tar from the fire can help to protect a thatched roof, and the smoke can keep out insects and other pests. Cooking habits need to be considered, as well as the lifestyle of the users. Light charcoal stoves used for

70

cooking meat and vegetables are of little use to people whose staple diets include food such as *Ugali*, which require large pots and vigorous stirring. Fuel type can differ greatly; in some countries cow dung is used as a common fuel source, particularly where wood is scarce. Cost is also a major factor among low-income groups. Failing to identify these key socio-economic issues will ensure that a stove programme will fail. The function of an improved stove is not merely to save fuel.

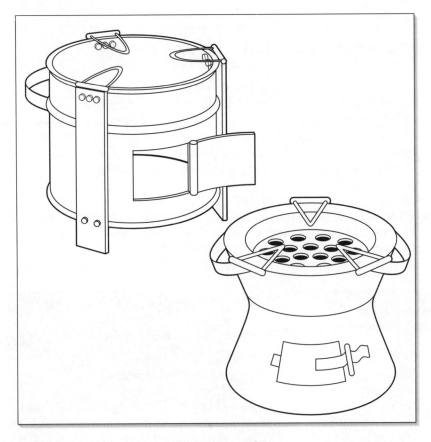

Figure 5.1: *A traditional metal stove and a KCJ*

Charcoal production
There are several methods of processing wood residues to make them cleaner and easier to use as well as easier to transport. Production of charcoal is the most common. It is worth mentioning at this point that the conversion of wood fuel to charcoal does not increase the energy content of the fuel – in fact the energy content is decreased. Charcoal is often produced in rural areas and transported for use in urban areas.

Charcoal is produced in a kiln or pit. A typical traditional earth kiln (see Figure 5.2) will comprise the fuel to be carbonized, which is stacked in a pile and

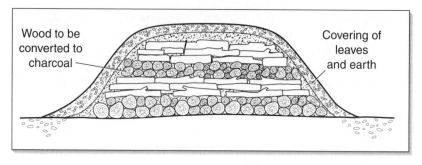

Figure 5.2: *A traditional earth kiln for charcoal production*

covered with a layer of leaves and earth. Once the combustion process is under way the kiln is sealed, and then only once the process is complete and cooling has taken place can the charcoal be removed. A simple improvement to the traditional kiln is shown in Figure 5.3. A chimney and air ducts have been introduced, which allow for a sophisticated gas and heat circulation system – and with very little capital investment a significant increase in yield is achieved.

Briquetting
Briquetting is the densification of loose biomass material. Many waste products, such as wood residues and sawdust from the timber industry, municipal waste, bagasse from sugar-cane processing, or charcoal dust are briquetted to increase compactness and transportability. Briquetting is often a large-scale commercial

Charcoal kiln, Kenya

Photograph: Intermediate Technology/Heinz Muller

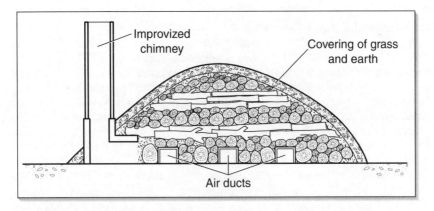

Figure 5.3: *Improved charcoal kiln found in Brazil, Sudan and Malawi*

activity and the raw material will be carbonized during the process to produce a usable gas and also a more user-friendly briquette. Some improved stoves have been designed specifically to be used with briquettes (Karekezi and Ranja, 1997).

Commercial utilization of biomass

Biomass can be used for a variety of commercial activities. There are several technologies that employ direct combustion of unprocessed or semi-processed biomass to produce process heat for a variety of end uses. The most common is the simple furnace and boiler system, which raises steam for applications such as tobacco curing, electricity generation and beer brewing. Biomass is also used to provide direct heat for brick burning, lime burning, sugar processing and cement kilns. The advantage of using biomass is that it is available locally, thereby avoiding shortages associated with poor fuel supply networks and fluctuating costs.

Other issues

Biomass energy and the environment

Initially, one environmental concern dominated the improved stoves work – saving trees. Today, this issue is considerably downplayed as time has brought a clearer understanding of the true causes of deforestation. At the same time, other environmental issues have become dominant – the household environment with its smoke, heat and lighting requirements, has been given greater consideration. These micro-environmental needs are often as complex as the broader environmental concerns, and this is reflected in the fact that no one improved stove design can meet the needs of a wide and diverse range of people.

Large-scale production of biomass can be carried out on an environmentally sustainable basis if care is taken to control the rate of extraction (for example from plantations of suitable trees that are cut back by coppicing (cutting back branches to the trunk) every few years, in rotation. Nutrients need to be replaced in the soil in these cases – for example from sewage waste. Continual large-scale exploitation of biomass resources without care for its replacement and regeneration will cause environmental damage and also jeopardize the fuel source itself.

Local manufacture of stoves

Since 1982, the Kenya Ceramic Jiko (KCJ), an improved charcoal-burning stove aimed at the urban market, has been developed and manufactured by large numbers of small producers. The KCJ has two main components – metal and ceramic (fired clay). Both these parts are made by entrepreneurs; the metal part (cladding) being made by small-scale enterprises or individual artisans, while the ceramic part (liner) is manufactured by slightly larger and more organized enterprises or women's groups. The KCJ is sold by the artisans directly to their customers or through commercial outlets such as retail shops and supermarkets. The stove was initially promoted heavily – to develop the market – by the NGO KENGO and by the Kenyan Ministry of Energy, through the mass media, market demonstrations and trade fairs.

As a result of this substantial promotion, there are now more than 200 artisans and micro-enterprises manufacturing some 13 600 improved stoves every month. It is estimated that there are now some 700 000 such stoves in use in Kenyan households. This represents a penetration of 16.8 per cent of all households in Kenya, and 56 per cent of all urban households in the country.

Source: Dominic Walubengo in Stove Images, *1995*

Woman making an improved cook stove
Photograph: Intermediate Technology/
Simon Ekless

Women, wood fuel, work and welfare

Collection of firewood is a major burden, which often falls to women, children and old people. The pressures on women's time are heavy, and cooking and fuel collection are among the most arduous of their tasks. The effects of inhaling smoke from burning wood during cooking are serious and are the subjects of current research; chronic bronchitis, heart disease, acute respiratory diseases and eye infections have been linked with smoky interiors. The impact of fuel shortage on cooking and nutrition are difficult to measure and are not given the attention they deserve.

As fuel shortages make extra demands on time and energy, women adapt their working patterns. More time spent collecting fuel can mean less time growing or preparing food, so that quality and quantity of food diminish. Malnourished women become more vulnerable to smoke pollution, which damages their lungs, eyes, children and unborn babies. But improved stoves can cook faster and burn fuel more efficiently, which lowers levels of exposure to biomass smoke and releases time for other activities. Adapting kitchen design can also help remove smoke from the cooking area.

Better choice of technology can help to emancipate women from drudgery and give them more control over precious resources. In some places, cooking is a particularly time-consuming task, so an improved stove that cooks faster may be very popular. Elsewhere, fuel management strategies by women save more fuel than carefully planned stove programmes. Stove designers can offer choices, but decisions about household energy technologies should be taken by women cooks, since they know what is needed for effective cooking, and what will be acceptable.

Biogas and liquid biofuels

Biomass residues can also be converted into various non-solid fuel forms. These fuels are referred to as biogas and liquid biofuels. The aim of this conversion process is to improve the quality, specific energy content and transportability of the raw biomass source, or to capture gases that are naturally produced as biomass is microbiologically degraded or when biomass is partially combusted. Biogas is a well-established fuel for cooking and lighting in a number of countries, while a major motivating factor in the development of liquid biofuels has been the drive to replace petroleum fuels. In this section we shall be looking at some of these fuels, their applications and the conversion technologies used to derive them.

Technical

Biogas
Biogas is produced by microbiological activity in the absence of air. It occurs naturally at the bottom of ponds and marshes and gives rise to methane, a combustible gas. There are two common man-made technologies for obtaining biogas, the first (which is more widespread) is the fermentation of human and/or animal waste in specially designed digesters. The second is a more recently developed technology for capturing methane from municipal waste landfill sites. The scale of simple biogas plants can vary from a small household system to large commercial plants of several thousand cubic metres.

The digestion of animal and human waste yields several benefits.

○ Methane is produced and can be used as a fuel.
○ The waste is reduced to slurry which has a high nutrient content which makes an ideal fertilizer; in some cases this fertilizer is the main product from the digester and the biogas is merely a by-product.
○ During the digestion process, bacteria in the manure are killed, which is a great benefit to environmental health.

Two popular simple designs of digester have been developed: the Chinese fixed dome digester and the Indian floating cover biogas digester (shown in Figures 5.4

75

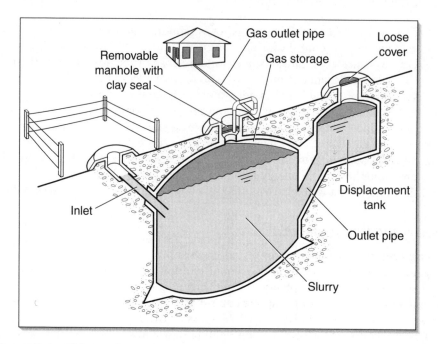

Figure 5.4: *Chinese fixed dome digester*

and 5.5). The digestion process is the same in both digesters, but the gas collection method is different in each. In the floating cover type, the water-sealed cover of the digester is capable of rising as gas is produced and acts as a storage chamber, whereas the fixed dome type has a lower gas storage capacity and requires good sealing if gas leakage is to be prevented. Both have been designed for use with animal waste or dung.

The waste is fed into the digester via the inlet pipe and undergoes digestion in the digestion chamber. The temperature of the process is quite critical – methane-producing bacteria operate most efficiently at temperatures between 30 and 40°C or 50 and 60°C – and in colder climates heat may have to be added to the chamber to encourage the bacteria to carry out their function. The product is a combination of methane and carbon dioxide, typically in the ratio of 6:4. Digestion time ranges from a couple of weeks to a couple of months depending on the feedstock and the digestion temperature. The residual slurry is removed at the outlet and can be used as a fertilizer.

Biogas has a variety of applications. Table 5.3 shows some typical applications for one cubic metre of biogas. Small-scale biogas digesters usually provide fuel for domestic lighting and cooking.

Some countries have initiated large-scale biogas programmes, Tanzania being an example. The Tanzanian model is based on integrated resource recovery from municipal and industrial waste for grid-based electricity and fertilizer production.

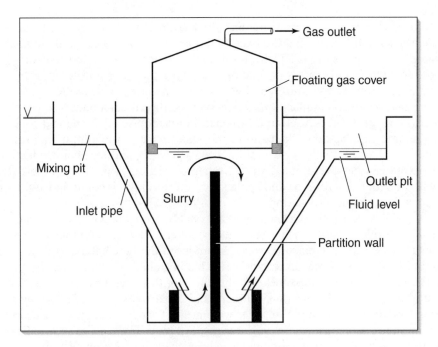

Figure 5.5: *Indian floating cover digester*

Table 5.3: Some biogas equivalents

Application	1m³ biogas equivalent
Lighting	Equal to 60–100 watt bulb for six hours
Cooking	Can cook three meals for a family of five or six
Fuel replacement	0.7kg of petrol
Shaft power	Can run a one horsepower motor for two hours
Electricity generation	Can generate 1.25 kilowatt hours of electricity

Source: Adapted from Kristoferson and Bokalders, 1991

Biomass gasification

The process of biomass gasification is distinctly different from that of biogas production. Gasification is the process by which solid biomass materials are broken down using heat to produce a combustible gas, commonly known as producer gas. Common feedstocks for combustion include wood, charcoal, rice husks and coconut shells.

The biomass gasification plant consists of a reactor, similar to a simple stove, into which the solid biomass fuel is fed. The supply of air to the fuel is, however, carefully controlled to allow only partial combustion of the fuel to take place. During this process gases are given off, which are captured and can be used as a gaseous fuel. Several combustible gases are given off – hydrogen, carbon monoxide and methane – as well as carbon dioxide and nitrogen.

Two reactor types exist: the fluidized-bed reactor which is used with large-scale gasification system, and the fixed-bed reactor which is employed for small-scale producer gas systems. There are three varieties of fixed-bed reactor: updraft, downdraft and crossdraft. Each reactor type produces a different ratio of gases at different temperatures, and with a differing level of cleanliness.

The gas has several applications. It can be used directly in a burner to provide process heat or it can be used in IC engines, but it requires cleaning and cooling for the latter application. Plant ratings for small-scale power output can range from several kilowatts up to several hundred kilowatts, and for heat production the output can be several megawatts. System efficiencies vary considerably depending on fuel, reactor type and application. Producer gas is commonly used for commercial cooking applications.

The small-scale gasifier technology is reasonably simple and cheap and can be manufactured locally, although care should be taken to ensure safety standards are maintained as carbon monoxide, which is produced during combustion, is a toxic gas. In China, a down-draught reactor design has been in production since the 1960s which uses rice husks as feedstock, and hundreds of these systems are in use. They have also been installed in Mali, Surinam and India (Stassen, 1995). During the Second World War, when fuel supplies were in short supply, millions of vehicles in Europe were adapted to run on producer gas, and today in countries such as Brazil and the Philippines gasifiers are commercially available for a variety of applications.

Liquid biofuels
Liquid biofuels, as their name suggests, are fuels derived from biomass and processed to produce a combustible liquid fuel. There are two main categories:

- o alcohol fuels – these include ethanol and methanol, and
- o vegetable oils – derived from plant seeds, such as sunflower, sesame, linseed and oilseed rape.

Ethanol is the most widely used liquid biofuel. It is an alcohol and is fermented from sugars, starches or from cellulosic biomass. Most commercial production of ethanol is from sugar cane or sugar beet, as starches and cellulosic biomass usually require expensive pre-treatment. It is used as a renewable energy fuel source as well as for the manufacture of cosmetics, pharmaceuticals and also for the production of alcoholic beverages.

Methanol is produced by a process of chemical conversion. It can be produced from any biomass with a moisture content of less than 60 per cent; potential feedstocks include forest and agricultural residues, wood and various energy crops. As with ethanol, it can either be blended with gasoline to improve the octane rating of the fuel or used in its neat form. Both ethanol and methanol are often preferred fuels for racing cars.

Vegetable oils. A further method of extracting energy from biomass is the production of vegetable oils as fuel. The process of oil extraction is carried out in

Source: Goldemberg et al., Renewable energy, sources for fuels and electricity, *1993*

the same way as for extraction of edible oil from plants. There are many crops grown in rural areas of the developing world which are suitable for oil production – coconut, cotton seed, groundnut, palm, rapeseed, soy bean and more.

There are two well-established technologies for oil extraction.

○ The simple screw press is a device for physically extracting the oil from the plant. This technology is well suited to small-scale production of oil as fuel or as foodstuff in rural areas. The press can be motorized or hand-operated.
○ Solvent extraction is a chemical process which requires large, sophisticated equipment. This method is more efficient – that is, it extracts a greater percentage of the oil from the plant – but is less suited to rural applications.

The oil, as well as being used for lighting and heating, can be used as a fuel in internal combustion engines. However, using pure vegetable oils (such as palm oil) can have adverse effects on diesel engines, such as the production of stalactites at the fuel injectors. Some vegetable oils, such as Jatropha (Physic Nut) give better performance. Mixes of vegetable oils and diesel can be run without harming engines, but there is concern about the health effects of exhaust gases from such mixes. As diesel engines may be run in enclosed spaces, this must be taken into account. Sunflower oil, for example, has an energy content about 85 per cent that of diesel fuel. There appears to be little uptake of this fuel as a source of energy so far.

Other issues

Present status
Small-scale biogas production in rural areas is now a well-established technology, particularly in countries such as China and India. At the end of 1993, about

79

five and a quarter million farmer households had biogas digesters, with an annual production of approximately 1.2 billion cubic metres of methane, as well as 3500kW installed capacity of biogas-fuelled electricity plant.

In India, there has been widespread development and dissemination of gasification technology to meet a variety of rural energy needs – for example, irrigation pumping and village electrification.

Ethanol production programmes have been initiated in several developing countries. The success of the Brazilian programme was mentioned earlier, while in Zimbabwe, for example, an annual production of about 40 million litres has been possible since 1983, using locally manufactured equipment.

Biomass energy and the environment

There are two areas of environmental concern when considering using biomass as a form of energy. First, there is the issue of land degradation and deforestation. This concern can be addressed by proper management of sustainable energy crops. Although much of the biomass requirement for energy production can be met by utilizing residues from the food industry, from agriculture or from commercial activity, careful planning of energy cropping is required to prevent undue stress on the environment.

Second, with the recent global call to reduce carbon dioxide emissions, there is a strong case for promoting the use of sustainable biomass-to-energy technologies worldwide. Using modern technology, significant reductions can be made in carbon dioxide emissions, particularly if liquid biofuels are used to replace their fossil-based equivalents. In fact, if biomass energy production is done on a sustainable basis, there is little net carbon dioxide addition to the environment.

There are other environmental concerns related to each fuel which need to be kept in mind, such as toxic emissions and the production of tars and soots.

Local manufacture and involvement

Many biomass conversion technologies for rural applications are easily manufactured by local artisans or by small and medium-sized engineering workshops. In Zimbabwe, locally made equipment for large-scale ethanol production has led to the lowest capital cost per litre for any ethanol plant in the world.

In China and India, biogas plants are produced in great numbers by local artisans. In Kenya, where biogas technology is still in its early stages of dissemination, local manufacturers have been quick to realize the potential and get involved with production of biogas plant.

Dissemination

Kenya relies on imported petroleum to meet 75 per cent of its commercial energy needs. In 1980, in an effort to reduce this high level of dependence on an externally controlled fuel source, the Kenyan government set up the Special Energy Programme (SEP). One aspect of the programme was the introduction and dissemination of biogas plant technology. After a poor start working with educational institutions the programme turned to local artisans and commercial outlets working in the private sector. Hands-on training was given to masons and plumbers, and private traders were encouraged to manufacture and stock appliances such as cookers and lights. By 1995, the number of plants installed in Kenya was estimated to be 880.

Wind pumping

Wind pumping for rural areas
There are manufacturers in several developing countries now producing wind pumps. The uptake of wind machines for water pumping, however, has been generally very slow even though the technology is well suited to the demands of many regions of Africa, Asia and Latin America. Where they are used, the demand is for one of the following end uses:

o village water supplies
o irrigation, or
o livestock water supplies.

Water pumping is one of the most basic and widespread energy needs in rural areas of the world. It has been estimated that half the world's rural population does not have access to clean water supplies.

Technical
(See also the Wind power for electricity generation section)

The power in the wind
The wind systems that exist over the earth's surface are a result of variations in air pressure. These are, in turn, due to the variations in solar heating. Warm air rises and cooler air rushes in to take its place. Wind is merely the movement of air from one place to another. There are global wind patterns related to large-scale solar heating of different regions of the earth's surface and seasonal variations in solar incidence. There are also localized wind patterns due the effects of temperature differences between land and seas, or mountains and valleys.

Wind speed data can be obtained from wind maps or from the meteorology office. Unfortunately, the general availability and reliability of wind speed data is extremely poor in many regions of the world. Significant areas of the world have mean wind speeds of above 3m/s, however, which makes the use of wind pumps an economically attractive option. It is important to obtain accurate wind speed data for the site before any decision can be made as to its suitability. Methods for assessing the mean wind speed are found in the relevant texts (see References and resources).

The power in the wind is proportional to:

o the area of windmill being swept by the wind
o the cube of the wind speed, and
o the air density – which varies with altitude.

The formula used for calculating the power in the wind is shown below:

$$P_w = \tfrac{1}{2}\,\rho\,A\,V^3$$

where P_w is power (in kilowatts) available in the wind
  ρ is the air density in kilograms per metre cubed
  A is the swept rotor area in square metres, and
  V is the wind speed in metres per second.

Wind into watts
Although the equation above gives us the power in the wind, the actual power that we can extract from the wind is significantly less than this figure. The actual power will depend on several factors, such as the type of machine and rotor used, the sophistication of blade design, friction losses, the losses in the pump or other equipment connected to the wind machine. There are also physical limits to the amount of power that can realistically be extracted from the wind. It can be shown theoretically that any windmill can only possibly extract a maximum of 59.3 per cent of the power from the wind (this is known as the Betz limit). In reality, for a wind pump, this figure is usually around 30 to 40 per cent, and for a large electricity producing turbine around 45 per cent maximum (see the description of Coefficient of performance on page 83).

So, modifying the formula for 'power in the wind' we can say that the power that is produced by the wind machine can be given by:

$$P_M = C_p\,\tfrac{1}{2}\,\rho\,A\,V^3$$

where P_M is power (in kilowatts) available from the machine, and
  C_p is the coefficient of performance of the wind machine.

It is also worth bearing in mind that a wind machine will operate at maximum efficiency for only a fraction of the time it is running, due to variations in wind speed. A rough estimate of the output from a wind pump can be obtained using the following equation;

$$P_A = 0.1\,A\,V^3$$

where P_A is the average power output in watts over the year, and
  V is the mean annual wind speed in metres per second.

Principles of wind energy conversion
There are two primary physical principles by which energy can be extracted from the wind; these are through the creation of either lift or drag force (or through a combination of the two). The difference between drag and lift is illustrated by the difference between using a spinnaker sail, which fills like a parachute and pulls a sailing boat with the wind, and a Bermuda rig – the familiar triangular sail which deflects the wind and allows a sailing boat to travel across the wind or slightly into the wind (see Figure 5.6).

Drag forces provide the most obvious means of propulsion, these being the forces felt by a person (or object) exposed to the wind. Lift forces are the most efficient means of propulsion, but being more subtle than drag forces are not so well understood.

The basic features that characterize lift and drag are:

- ○ drag is in the direction of air flow
- ○ lift is perpendicular to the direction of air flow
- ○ generation of lift always causes a certain amount of drag to be developed
- ○ with a good aerofoil, the lift produced can be more than thirty times greater than the drag, and
- ○ lift devices are generally more efficient than drag devices.

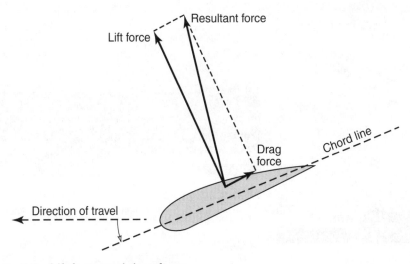

Figure 5.6: *Lift force and drag force*
Source: Spera, David A., *Wind Turbine Technology*, 1994

Types and characteristics of rotors

There are two main families of wind machines: vertical axis machines and horizontal axis machines. These, in turn, can use either lift or drag forces to harness the wind. The horizontal axis lift device is the type most commonly used. In fact, other than a few experimental machines, virtually all windmills come under this category.

There are several technical parameters that are used to characterize windmill rotors. The *tip-speed ratio* is defined as the ratio of the speed of the extremities of a windmill rotor to the speed of the free wind. Drag devices always have tip-speed ratios of less than one and hence turn slowly, whereas lift devices can have high tip-speed ratios (up to 13:1) and hence turn quickly relative to the wind.

The proportion of the power in the wind that the rotor can extract is termed the *coefficient of performance* (or power coefficient or efficiency; symbol C_p) and its variation as a function of tip-speed ratio is commonly used to characterize different types of rotor. As mentioned earlier, there is an upper limit of $C_p = 59.3$

per cent, although in practice real wind rotors have maximum C_p values in the range of 25–45 per cent.

Solidity is usually defined as the percentage of the area of the rotor that contains material rather than air. High-solidity machines carry a lot of material and have blade angles. They generate much higher starting torque (torque is the twisting or rotary force produced by the rotor) than low-solidity machines, but are inherently less efficient. The wind pump is generally of this type. Low-solidity machines tend to be used for electricity generation. High solidity machines will have a low tip-speed ratio, and vice versa. The choice of rotor is dictated largely by the characteristic of the load, and hence of the end use.

High-solidity rotor
Photograph: Intermediate Technology/Teresa Anderson

Low-solidity rotor
Photograph: Intermediate
Technology

Water pumping

Matching rotor and pump

When installing a wind pump it is important to match the characteristics of the pump and the wind machine. A good interaction between pump and rotor is essential. The most common type of pump used for water pumping (especially for borehole water pumping) in conjunction with a windmill is the reciprocating or piston pump. The piston pump tends to have a high torque requirement on starting because, when starting, the rotor has to provide enough torque to overcome the weight of the pump rods and water in the rising main – once the rotor is turning, the torque requirement decreases because of the momentum of the revolving rotor. The wind speed can then drop to about two-thirds of the start-up wind speed before the wind pump will stop.

Other common pump types used for wind pumping are the progressive cavity or 'Mono' pump and the centrifugal pump. Both have advantages in certain circumstances, but both also tend to be expensive and less commonly used.

84

A typical example of a modern multi-bladed wind pump can be seen in the photograph of the high-solidity rotor. The high solidity means high starting and running torque and low running speed, which is desirable for use with the piston pump.

It is obviously important to match the wind pump size with the demand for water and the available wind and hence decide upon a suitable rotor size. To calculate the demand we need to know the following data:

○ the head to which the water is to be pumped – in metres, and
○ the volume of water to be pumped per day – in metres cubed.

For water at sea level the approximate energy requirement can be calculated using the following equation:

$$E = 0.002725 \times \text{volume} \times \text{head} \quad \text{(in kilowatt-hours)}$$

Typically, pumping heads can vary between a few metres and 100m (and occasionally more), while the volume of water required can vary from a few cubic metres a day for domestic use to a few hundred cubic metres for irrigation.

Anatomy of a wind pump
A borehole is by far the most common water source from which the wind pump will draw water. A classic multiblade farm wind pump has a piston pump pumping to an elevated storage tank. There are many other configurations possible, depending on the nature of the water source and the demand. These machines usually have rotor diameters of between 1.5 and 8 metres, and seldom exceed 4 or 5 metres. The power is transmitted from the rotor to the pump rods via a gearing system or via a direct drive mechanism. The movement of the pump rods causes the pump to lift water to the tank. Water can then be fed into the distribution network from the tank. The function of the tail vane is to keep the rotor oriented into the wind. Most wind pumps have a tail vane which is designed for automatic furling (turning the machine out of the wind) at high wind speeds to prevent damage.

Wind pumping with electricity
Although the multiblade wind pump is by far the most common wind pump in use, it is not the only option available. Another option, especially where there is a requirement for the pump to be sited remote from the wind machine, is to use an aerogenerator to provide electricity for an electric pump. Although they tend to be more expensive, they do have the advantage that the electricity can be used for other applications when not pumping, and also that the electricity can be stored in batteries for use when the wind speed is insufficient for direct electricity supply.

Other issues

Local manufacture
Wind pumps are manufactured in small numbers in various countries throughout the world. There are manufacturers producing wind pumps in Europe, Australia, South Africa and the USA for export, but there are also commercial enterprises in developing countries manufacturing wind pumps. One such manufacturer, the Rural Industries and Innovations Centre (RIIC) in Botswana, is mentioned on page 87.

There have been several projects over the last couple of decades with the aim of transferring wind pump technology to manufacturers in the South, and there has been some success. One such success story is the Kijito wind pump manufactured in Kenya. This wind pump was originally developed by the Intermediate Technology Development Group (ITDG) based in the UK, in conjunction with a local manufacturer in Kenya. The Kijito design has been further developed and about 25 wind pumps a year are produced. An almost identical design is also being made by a local manufacturer in Harare, Zimbabwe.

The Kijito windpump

Photograph: Intermediate Technology

The table below shows the cost comparison for the most common pumping options.

Table 5.4: Cost comparison of water pumping options

	Diesel	*Wind*	*Solar*
Capital cost	$1500	$2000	$8000
Storage tank*	$250	$600	$450
Total annual cost	$600	$400	$1300
Cost per m³	¢12	¢7.5	¢25

Example: for irrigating 0.5 ha with a water table depth of 4m, total water demand over 1 year = 5000m³
*For diesel pumps, which can be operated when water is needed, a tank is necessary for fuel storage. For wind and solar applications, when it is best to pump water whenever the resource is available, the water must be stored in a tank until needed.

User perspective – wind pumps in Botswana

A survey of owners/users of wind pumps was conducted in Botswana. The aim was to determine the ownership, procurement and installation, use, environmental impact and the promotional plan. The survey revealed that 54 per cent of the wind pumps were owned by households and 23 per cent by farmers' groups or syndicates. The rest (23 per cent) were owned by the community. The majority of the wind pumps (85 per cent) were purchased and the rest were donated. Fifty-six per cent of the respondents purchased wind pumps or raised the money from the banks to purchase them, whereas 18 per cent utilized group contributions. Most of the respondents purchased the wind pumps from RIIC, the local supplier. The installation of the wind pumps was done by RIIC in 69 per cent of the cases, and by owners and foreign dealers in 23 per cent and 8 per cent of the cases, respectively.

Thirty-one per cent depended entirely on wind pumps for their water pumping, while 69 per cent had other systems. The respondents perceived wind pumps as a good technology, mainly because they were cheaper to use. One of the problems associated with the use of wind pumps was the high incidence of breakdowns. Forty-six per cent indicated that they broke down once a year, 31 per cent twice a year and 23 per cent more than three times a year. Major repairs were done by the supplier (54 per cent), local technicians (8 per cent) or a combination of the two (8 per cent).

The study also investigated the perception of respondents of the environmental impact of the use of wind pumps. The majority (85 per cent) thought the wind pumps improved the scenery, whereas 15 per cent said they do not make a difference. No negative impacts were reported. It was also the view of 92 per cent of the respondents that the noise from the wind pumps is not a nuisance. The respondents thought that the adoption of the wind pump technology was constrained by factors such as the lack of appropriate policies, lack of awareness of the technology, high costs of maintenance and inadequate wind regimes.

Wind power for electricity generation

Modern wind generators

Modern wind turbine generators are highly sophisticated machines using the latest materials and production techniques. Led by improvements in aerodynamic and structural design, materials technology and mechanical, electrical and control engineering, they are capable of producing up to a megawatt or more of electricity from each machine. Wind power is now an economically attractive option for commercial electricity generation in the right conditions. Large wind farms or wind power stations have become a common sight in many countries.

To a lesser degree, there has been a parallel development in small-scale wind generators for supplying electricity for battery charging, for stand-alone applications and for connection to small grids. Table 5.5 shows the classification system for wind turbines.

The power in the wind

There are global wind patterns related to large-scale solar heating of different regions of the earth's surface, and seasonal variations in solar incidence. There are also localized wind patterns due to the effects of temperature differences between land and seas, or mountains and valleys. Wind speed generally increases with height above ground. This is because the roughness of ground features such as vegetation and houses cause the wind to be slowed.

Anatomy and characteristics of the wind generator

A typical small wind generator has a rotor that is directly coupled to a generator which produces electricity either at 120/240V alternating current for direct domestic use, or at 12/24V direct current for battery charging. Larger machines generate 3-phase electricity. There is often a tail vane which keeps the rotor oriented into the

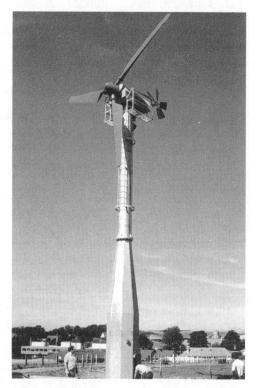

Wind power generators are now common worldwide

Photograph: Intermediate Technology

Table 5.5: Classification for system for wind turbines

Scale	Rotor diameter	Power rating
Micro	Less than 3m	Battery charging, 50W up to 1–2kW
Small	Less than 12m	
Medium	12m to 45m	Less than 40kW
Large	46m and larger	40kW to more than 1.0MW

wind. Some wind machines have a tail vane which is designed for automatic furling (turning the machine out of the wind) at high wind speeds to prevent damage. Larger machines have pitch controlled blades (the angle at which the blades meet the wind is controlled) which achieves the same function. The tower is of low solidity to prevent wind interference and is often guyed to give support to the tower.

The specifications for a typical small wind turbine are shown in Table 5.6.

Table 5.6: Details for BWC 1500, Bergey Windpower Co., USA

Type	3 blade upwind
Rotor diameter	3.0 metres
Drive	Direct
Rated power	1500 watts
Start-up wind speed	3.6m/s
Cut-in wind speed	3.6m/s
Rated wind speed	12.5m/s
Furling wind speed	14.3m/s
Maximum design wind speed	53.6m/s
Overspeed protection	AUTOFURL™
Generator	Permanent magnet alternator
Output form	3-phase a.c. variable frequency or 12V–24V d.c.

Source: Bergey Windpower Catalogue

Grid connected or battery charging
In areas where households are widely dispersed or where grid costs are prohibitively expensive, battery charging is an option. For people in rural areas a few tens of watts of power is sufficient for providing lighting and a source of power for a radio or television. Batteries can be returned to the charging station occasionally for recharging. This reduces the inconvenience of an intermittent supply due to fluctuating windspeeds. There are 12V and 24V direct current wind generators commercially available which are suitable for battery-charging applications. Smaller turbines (50–150 watts) are available for individual household connections.

Other issues

Cost – economics
The cost of producing electricity from the wind is heavily dependent on the local wind regime. As

Typical small wind turbine
Photograph: Intermediate Technology

89

mentioned earlier, the power output from the wind machine is proportional to the cube of the windspeed and so a slight increase in windspeed will mean a significant increase in power and a subsequent reduction in unit costs.

Capital costs for wind power are high, but running costs are low and so access to initial funds, subsidies or low-interest loans are an obvious advantage when considering a wind-electric system. A careful matching of the load and energy supply options should be made to maximize the use of the power from the wind – a load which accepts a variable input is ideally matched to the intermittent nature of wind power.

Larger wind farms can generate grid electricity without harmful environmental effects
Photograph: Intermediate Technology

Local manufacture

Depending on the availability of materials, rotor blades can be made locally from laminated wood, steel, plastics or combinations of these materials, while some of the machinery components can be made by small engineering workshops. Other parts, including special bearings, gearboxes, generators and other electrical equipment may have to be imported if they are not available in the country of assembly. Towers can be made of welded steel, preferably galvanized, which can be manufactured in many local engineering works, while the foundations can be cast from reinforced concrete on site. (Source: Kristoferson and Bokalders, 1991.)

Micro-hydro power

Water can be harnessed on a large or a small scale. Table 5.7 outlines the categories that are used to define power output from hydro power. Micro-hydro power is the small-scale harnessing of energy from falling water; for example, harnessing enough water from a local river to power a small factory or village. This section will concentrate mainly on micro-hydro power.

Table 5.7: Classification of hydro-power by size

Large hydro	More than 100MW and usually feeding into a large electricity grid
Medium hydro	15–100MW – usually feeding into a grid
Small hydro	1–15MW – usually feeding into a grid
Mini-hydro	Above 100kW, but below 1MW; either stand-alone schemes or more often feeding into a grid
Micro-hydro	Ranging from a few hundred watts for battery charging or food processing applications up to 100kW; usually provide power for a small community or rural industry in remote areas away from the grid

kW (kilowatt) = 1000 watts; MW (megawatt) = 1 000 000 watts or 1000kW

Micro-hydro scheme in Nepal

Over the last few decades there has been a growing realization in developing countries that micro-hydro schemes have an important role to play in the economic development of remote rural areas, especially mountainous ones. Micro-hydro schemes can provide power for industrial, agricultural and domestic uses through direct mechanical power or by coupling the turbine to a generator to produce electricity.

Technical

Scheme components

Figure 5.7 shows the main components of a run-of-the-river micro-hydro scheme. This type of scheme requires no water storage, but instead diverts some of the water from the river, which is channelled along the side of a valley before being 'dropped' into the turbine via a penstock. The turbine drives a generator which provides electricity for a workshop. The transmission line can be extended to a local village to supply domestic power for lighting and other uses.

There are various other configurations that can be used, depending on the topographical and hydrological conditions, but all adopt the same general principle.

Water into watts

To determine the power potential of the water flowing in a river or stream it is necessary to determine both the flow rate of the water and the head through which the water can be made to fall.

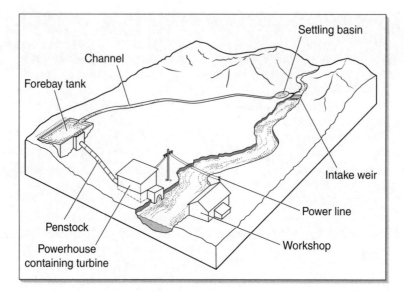

Figure 5.7: *Layout of a typical micro-hydro scheme*

theoretical power (P) is proportional to flow rate (Q) × head units (H)

The actual power is always less than the theoretical power available because of losses in the turbine and generator and friction losses in the pipework.

Example: A turbine generator set operating at a head of 10 metres with flow of 0.3 cubic metres per second will deliver approximately (9.81 × 0.5 × 0.3 × 10) = 15 kilowatts of electricity.

If a machine is operated under conditions other than full load or full flow then other significant inefficiencies must be considered. Part flow and part load characteristics of the equipment need to be known to assess the performance under these conditions. It is always preferable to run all equipment at the rated design flow and load conditions, but it is not always practical or possible where river flow fluctuates throughout the year or where daily load patterns vary considerably.

Depending on the end-use requirements of the generated power, the output from the turbine shaft can be used directly as mechanical power or the turbine can be connected to an electrical generator to produce electricity. For many rural industrial applications (for food processing such as milling or oil extraction, for a sawmill or carpentry workshop, or for small-scale mining equipment) shaft power is suitable, but many applications require conversion to electrical power. For domestic applications electricity is preferred. This can be provided either:

○ directly to the home via a small electrical distribution system, or
○ by means of batteries which are returned periodically to the power house for recharging. This system is common where the cost of direct electrification is prohibitive due to scattered housing (and hence an expensive distribution system).

Conditions suitable for micro-hydro power

The best geographical areas for exploiting small-scale hydro power are those where there are steep rivers flowing all year round; for example, the hill areas of countries with high year-round rainfall, or the great mountain ranges and their foothills, like the Andes and the Himalayas. Islands with moist marine climates, such as in the Caribbean, the Philippines and Indonesia are also suitable. Low-head turbines have been developed for small-scale exploitation of rivers where there is a small head but sufficient flow to provide adequate power.

To assess the suitability of a potential site, the hydrology of the site needs to be known and a site survey carried out to determine actual flow and head data. Hydrological information can be obtained from the meteorology or irrigation department usually run by the national government. These data give a good overall picture of annual rainfall patterns and likely fluctuations in rainfall and, therefore, flow patterns. The site survey gives more detailed information of the site conditions for power calculation and to allow design work to begin. Flow data should be gathered over a period of at least one full year, where possible, so as to ascertain the fluctuation in river flow over the various seasons. There are many methods of carrying out flow and head measurements and these can be found in the relevant texts (see References and Resources).

Turbines

A turbine converts the energy in falling water into shaft power. There are various types of turbine, which can be categorized in one of several ways. The choice of turbine will depend mainly on the pressure head available and the design flow for the proposed hydro-power installation. Turbines are broadly divided into three groups; high, medium and low head, and into two categories: impulse and reaction. The type of turbine is chosen based on the head available, and the size then depends on the water flow.

Load factor

The load factor is the ratio of power generated to power that could have been generated if the turbine were used continuously. Unlike technologies relying on costly fuel sources, the 'fuel' for hydro power generation is free and therefore the plant becomes more cost effective if run for a high percentage of the time. If the turbine is used only for domestic lighting in the evenings then the load factor will be very low and the cost cannot be justified. If the turbine provides power for rural industry during the day and meets domestic demand during the evening, then the level of use will be constant. It is very important to ensure a constant level of use, if the scheme is to be cost effective, and this should be taken into account during the planning stage.

Load control governors

Water turbines, like petrol or diesel engines, will vary in speed as load is applied or relieved. Although not such a great problem with machinery that uses direct shaft power, this speed variation will seriously affect both frequency and voltage output from a generator. Traditionally, complex hydraulic or mechanical speed governors altered the flow as the load varied, but more recently electronic load controllers (ELC) have been developed, which has increased the simplicity and reliability of modern micro-hydro sets. ELC prevent speed variations by continuously adding or subtracting an artificial load so that, in effect, the turbine is working permanently under full load. A further benefit is that an ELC has no moving parts, is very reliable and virtually maintenance free. The advent of electronic load control has allowed the introduction of simple and efficient multi-jet turbines, no longer burdened by expensive hydraulic governors.

Other issues

The economics – cost reduction

Normally, small-scale hydro installations in rural areas can offer considerable financial benefits to the communities served, particularly where careful planning identifies income-generating uses for the power. The major cost of a scheme is for site preparation and the capital cost of equipment. In general, unit cost decreases with a larger plant and with high heads of water. It could be argued that small-scale hydro technology does not bring with it the advantages of 'economy of scale', but many costs normally associated with larger hydro schemes have been 'designed out' or 'planned out' of micro-hydro systems to bring the unit cost in line with bigger schemes. This includes such innovations as:

- using run-of-the-river schemes where possible – this does away with the cost of an expensive dam for water storage
- using locally manufactured equipment where possible and appropriate
- using HDPE (plastic) penstocks where appropriate
- using an electronic load controller, which allows the power plant to be left unattended, thereby reducing labour costs, and introduces useful by-products such as battery charging or water heating as dump loads for surplus power; also does away with bulky and expensive mechanical control gear
- using existing infrastructure; for example, a canal which serves an irrigation scheme
- siting of power close to village to avoid expensive high voltage distribution equipment such as transformers
- using pumps as turbines (PAT) – in some circumstances standard pumps can be used 'in reverse' as turbines; this reduces costs, delivery time, and makes for simple installation and maintenance
- using motors as generators – as with the PAT idea, motors can be run 'in reverse' and used as generators; pumps are usually purchased with a motor fitted and the whole unit can be used as a turbine/generator set
- using local materials for the civil works
- using of community labour
- planning for a high plant factor (see above) and well-balanced load pattern (energy demand fluctuation throughout the day)

- using low-cost connections for domestic users, and
- using self-cleaning intake screens – this is a recent innovation which is fitted to the intake weir and prevents stones and silt from entering the headrace canal; this does away with the need for overspill and desilting structures along the headrace canal and also means that, in many cases, the canal can be replaced by a low-pressure conduit buried beneath the ground – this technology is, at present, still in its early stages of dissemination.

Maintenance costs (including insurance and water abstraction charges, where they apply) are a comparatively minor component of the total – although they may be an important consideration in marginal economic cases. For further details of the economics of micro-hydro power, see the case study on Chalan in Part III.

Micro-hydro can provide mechanical power for milling

Photograph: Intermediate Technology

Ownership and management
Programmes promoting the use of micro-hydro power in developing countries have concentrated on the social, as well as the technical and economic aspects of this energy source. Technology transfer and capacity building programmes have enabled local design and manufacture to be adopted. Local management, ownership and community participation has meant that many schemes are under the control of local people who own, run and maintain them. Operation and maintenance is usually carried out by trained local craftspeople.

Solar photovoltaic energy

Solar photovoltaic (PV) energy conversion turns sunlight directly into electricity. PV systems have an important use in areas remote from an electricity grid, where they provide power for water pumping, lighting, vaccine refrigeration, electrified livestock fencing, telecommunications and many other applications. Some tens of thousands of systems are currently in use but this number is insignificant compared to the vast potential that exists for PV as an energy source.

Photovoltaic modules provide an independent reliable electrical power source at the point of use, making them particularly suited to remote locations. PV systems

Array of PV panels

Photograph: Intermediate Technology/Smail Khennas

are technically viable and, with the recent reduction in production costs and increase in conversion efficiencies, can be economically feasible for many applications.

The use of PV electricity

Solar PV is particularly applicable in tropical regions where there is little seasonal variation in insolation level even during the rainy season. This means that, unlike northern industrial countries, solar energy can be harnessed economically throughout the year.

Over the decade 1984–94, the worldwide installed PV capacity increased dramatically. It is worth highlighting that the pattern of growth was almost the same in developed and developing countries. In Europe, for example, the installed capacity, which was only 3.75MW in 1984 reached 60.5MW in 1994; i.e. the production increased by a factor in excess of 16 during this decade. In Latin America the production was 1.4MW in 1984 and 32.2MW in 1994, i.e. a 23-fold increase during the decade. The pie chart (Figure 5.8) showing the type of applications for which PV was used between 1992 and 1994 indicates the importance of the market in developing countries. Applications such as water pumping, village power, solar home systems and other remote household uses account for 42 per cent of the total installed capacity world-wide.

Technical

The nature and availability of solar radiation

Solar radiation arrives on the surface of the earth at a maximum power density of approximately 1 kilowatt per square metre. The actual usable radiation

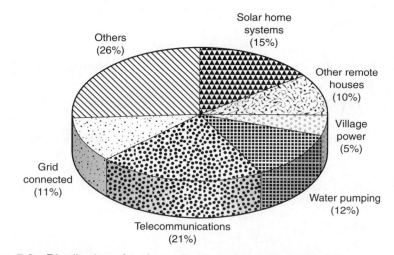

Figure 5.8: *Distribution of main applications (average 1992–94)*
Source: 'After photovoltaics in 2010', European Commission, Brussels, 1996

component varies depending on geographical location, cloud cover and hours of sunlight each day. As might be expected, the total solar radiation is highest at the equator, especially in sunny, desert areas.

Solar radiation arrives at the earth's outer atmosphere in the form of a direct beam. This light is then partially scattered by cloud, smog, dust or other atmospheric phenomena (Figure 5.9). We therefore receive solar radiation either as *direct* radiation, or scattered or *diffuse* radiation – the ratio depending on the atmospheric conditions. Both direct and diffuse components of radiation are useful, the only distinction between the two being that diffuse radiation cannot be concentrated for use.

The geometry of earth, sun and collector panel
The earth revolves around the sun with its axis tilted at an angle of 23.5 degrees. It is this tilt that gives rise to the seasons. The value of solar flux density is dependent upon the angle at which it strikes the earth's surface and so, as this angle changes during the yearly cycle, so the amount of sunshine changes. Thus, in northern countries, in the depths of winter, the sun will be low in the sky to the south, or may not even be seen at all in arctic regions. The radiation strikes the earth's surface obliquely and solar gain (solar yield) is low. If we are using a solar photovoltaic panel to capture the sun's energy then the orientation of this panel is also critical to the amount of energy we shall capture. The relationship is complex, and only with sophisticated tracking systems can the maximum energy be extracted for any given location.

The PV cell, modules and arrays
When light falls on the active surface, the electrons in a solar cell become energized, in proportion to the intensity and spectral distribution (wavelength distribution) of the light. When their energy level exceeds a certain point a potential difference is established across the cell. This is then capable of driving a current through an external load.

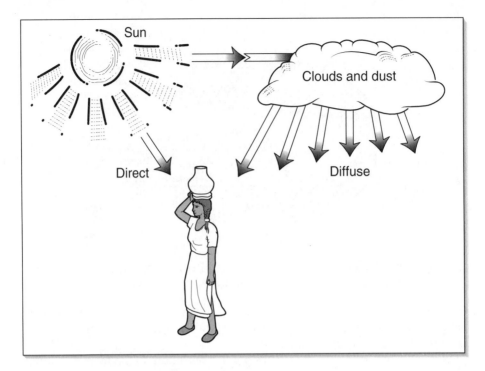

Figure 5.9: *Direct and diffuse solar radiation*

All modern commercial PV devices use silicon as the base material, mainly as mono-crystalline or multi-crystalline cells, but more recently also in amorphous form. A mono-crystalline silicon cell is made from a thin wafer of a high-purity silicon crystal, doped with a minute quantity of boron. Phosphorus is diffused into the active surface of the wafer. At the front, electrical contact is made by a metallic grid; at the back, contact usually covers the whole surface. An anti-reflective coating is applied to the front surface. Typical cell size is about 15cm in diameter.

Solar cells are interconnected in series and in parallel to achieve the desired operating voltage and current. They are then protected by encapsulation between glass and a tough resin back. This is held together by a stainless steel or aluminium frame to form a *module*. These modules, usually containing about 30 PV cells, form the basic building block of a *solar array*. Modules may be connected in series or in parallel to increase the voltage and current, and thus achieve the required solar array characteristics that will match the load. Typical module size is 50Wp, which produces direct current electricity at 12V (for battery charging, for example).

The process of producing efficient solar cells is costly due to the use of expensive pure silicon and the energy consumed but, as materials technology improves, costs are slowly dropping, making PV technology more attractive (see

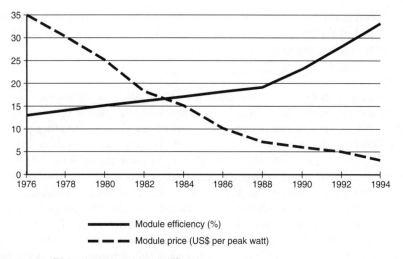

—— Module efficiency (%)

– – – Module price (US$ per peak watt)

Figure 5.10: *PV price trend and efficiency*

Figure 5.10). Cost has been the major barrier to the widespread uptake of PV technology. PV modules are usually priced in terms of peak watt (Wp), which is the power rating of the panel at peak conditions – that is, at $1kWm^{-2}$.

Commercially available modules fall into three types, based on the solar cells used.

- ○ Mono-crystalline cell modules. The highest cell efficiencies of around 15 per cent are obtained with these modules. The cells are cut from a mono-crystalline silicon crystal.
- ○ Multi-crystalline cell modules. The cell manufacturing process is lower in cost, but cell efficiencies of only around 12 per cent are achieved. A multi-crystalline cell is cut from a cast ingot of multi-crystalline silicon and is generally square in shape.
- ○ Amorphous silicon modules. These are made from thin films of amorphous silicon where efficiency is much lower (6–9 per cent) but the process uses less material. The potential for cost reduction is greatest for this type and much work has been carried out in recent years to develop amorphous silicon technology. Unlike mono-crystalline and multi-crystalline cells, with amorphous silicon there is some degradation of power output with time.

An array can vary from one or two modules with an output of 10W or less, to a vast bank of several kilowatts or even megawatts.

- ○ Flat plate arrays, which are held fixed at a tilted angle and face towards the equator, are most common. The angle of tilt should be approximately equal to the angle of latitude for the site. A steeper angle increases the output in winter; a shallower angle produces more output in summer. The angle of tilt should be at least 10 degrees to allow for rain runoff.
- ○ Tracking arrays follow the path of the sun during the day and thus theoretically capture more sun. However, the increased complexity and cost of the equipment rarely makes it worthwhile.

o Mobile (portable) arrays can be of use if the equipment being operated is required in different locations, such as with some lighting systems or small irrigation pumping systems.

Solar PV systems

PV systems are most commonly used for stand-alone applications. They can either be used to drive a load directly to pump water during the hours of sunlight and store it for later use, for example; or a battery can be used to store power for use for lighting during the evening. If a battery charging system is used then electronic control apparatus will be needed to monitor the system. All the components other than the PV module are referred to as the balance-of-system (BOS) components. Below, in Figure 5.11, three possible configurations of stand-alone PV systems are shown. Such systems can often be bought as kits and installed by semi-skilled labour. (Hulscher, W. and Fraenkel, P. 1994).

For correct sizing of PV systems the user needs to estimate the demand on the system, as well as acquiring information about the amount of sunshine in the

a) System without batteries

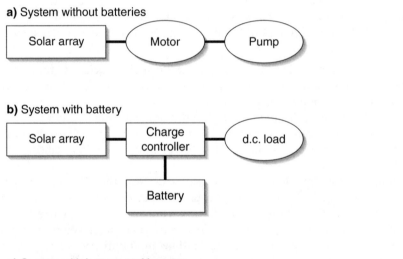

b) System with battery

c) System with battery and inverter

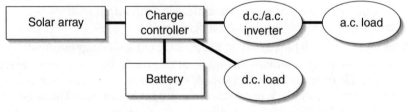

Figure 5.11: *Common configurations of PV systems*

100

area (approximations can be made if no data are readily available). It is normally assumed that for each Wp of rated power the module should provide 0.85 watt-hours of power for each kWhm^{-2} per day of sunshine. Therefore, if we consider a module rated at 200Wp and the amount of sunshine for our site is 5kWhm^{-2} per day (a typical value for tropical regions), then our system will produce 850Wh per day (that is $200 \times 0.85 \times 5 = 850$).

Some systems use lenses or mirrors to concentrate direct solar radiation on to smaller areas of solar cells. As the power output is directly proportional to the solar power directed on to the PV cell, this method is useful for reducing the area required for collection. The cost of the concentrators, however, often offsets the cost savings made on reducing the size of the module.

Some benefits of photovoltaics

Advantages	Disadvantages
Reliable – better than diesel	Difficult to repair if damaged
Low maintenance, easy to maintain	BOS components add to costs
Long life of panels, no moving parts	Batteries need to be looked after
No need to import fuel	Panels mostly imported – high capital cost
Low environmental impact	Can be easily stolen
Safe – no heat, noise, pollution	

PV can be used to power water pumping systems

Photograph: Intermediate Technology

PV applications in rural areas
1. Rural electrification

   o lighting and power supplies for remote buildings (mosques, churches, temples farms, schools, mountain refuge huts) – low wattage fluorescent lighting is recommended
   o power supplies for remote villages
   o street lighting
   o individual house systems
   o battery charging
   o mini-grids

2. Water pumping and treatment systems

   o pumping for drinking water
   o pumping for irrigation
   o dewatering and drainage
   o ice production

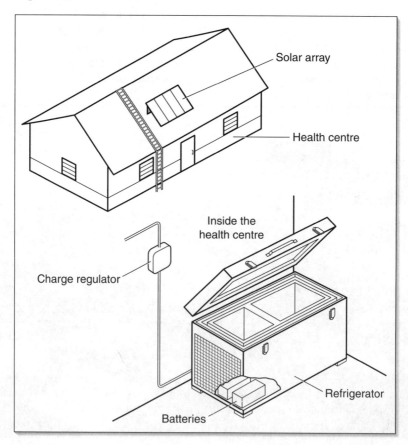

Figure 5.12: *PV is frequently used to power vaccine refrigeration in remote health centres*

- o saltwater desalination systems
- o water purification

3. Health care systems

  - o lighting in rural clinics
  - o UHF transceivers between health centres
  - o vaccine refrigeration
  - o ice pack freezing for vaccine carriers
  - o sterilizers
  - o blood storage refrigerators

4. Communications

  - o radio repeaters
  - o remote TV and radio receivers
  - o remote weather measuring
  - o rural telephone kiosks

5. Transport aids

  - o road sign lighting, hazard and warning lights
  - o railway crossings and signals
  - o navigation buoys
  - o road markers

6. Security systems

  - o security lighting
  - o remote alarm system
  - o electric fences

7. Miscellaneous

  - o ventilation systems
  - o calculators
  - o pumping and automated feeding systems on fish farms
  - o solar water heater circulation pumps
  - o boat/ship power
  - o vehicle battery trickle chargers
  - o earthquake monitoring systems
  - o emergency power for disaster relief

Other issues

Manufacturing – location

PV technology is sophisticated and the manufacturing plant is expensive. There are, however, large-scale manufacturers of PV modules working in India. For example, Central Electronics of Ghaziabad is not only the nation's largest PV producer, but is the fifth largest producer of monocrystalline silicon solar cells in the world. There are over 60 companies in India alone producing solar cells, modules and systems.

There is a vast scope and potential for the use of PV technology in India. There are still over 90 000 villages in the country to be electrified. Recognizing the importance of PV technology in the Indian context, the government has been implementing a comprehensive programme covering R&D, demonstration, commercialization and utilization for more than 15 years.

Among the elements of the action plan are the following aims:

○ deployment of 400 000 solar lanterns as a substitute for kerosene lanterns
○ rural electrification through PV systems covering 400 villages and hamlets
○ a special programme on water pumping systems
○ intensified R&D on technologies that can lead to a reduction in cost
○ commercialization of PV systems for various applications by giving a market orientation to the programme and promoting manufacturing and related activities.

As a result of these measures, India is among the leading countries in the world in the development and use of PV technology.

Source: E.V.R. Sastry, cited in Garg et al., Renewable Energy Technologies, Indian Institute of Technology and the British High Commission, *1997*

Hybrid systems
Solar PV systems can be used in conjunction with other energy technologies to provide an integrated, flexible system for remote power generation. These systems are referred to as hybrid systems. Common configurations of hybrid systems could include a solar PV array, wind generator and diesel generator set, which would allow generation in all weather conditions. Such systems need careful planning and can be complex to operate and maintain, since they involve several technologies and are expensive to buy.

Solar lanterns
A recent innovation in solar technology is the solar lantern. Originally designed for the outdoor leisure market in Western countries, this simple lantern with a small PV module (5–10 watts) is extremely appropriate to use in rural areas of developing countries for replacing kerosene lamps. While the cost has been a barrier, mass production of better lantern designs is set to bring the lanterns within reach of most hurricane lamp users. The batteries can be made in most countries that make automotive batteries, and the electronic regulators and casings can also be made in most countries with a modest industrial base. The advantages include affordability and the lack of any need for subsidy.

Micro-grids or stand-alone
Solar PV technology is presently best suited to stand-alone applications but can also be used to provide power for small grid systems with centralized power

generation. As the cost of PV cell production drops, their use for medium-scale electricity production is likely to be adopted more widely. There is also scope for eventual large-scale electricity production for such applications as peak power provision.

Table 5.8: Solar irradiation of selected areas in developing countries (average figures)

Coastal Africa	4kWh/m²/day
North Africa	5kWh/m²/day
Sahel	6kWh/m²/day

The variability of solar irradiation (see Table 5.8) is an important aspect of solar energy because it influences system design and solar energy economics. The output and the costs of a module of 50Wp will vary dramatically according to the amount of sunshine (see Table 5.9).

Table 5.9: Output relative to insolation for a 50Wp panel

Insolation (kW/m²/day)	Output (Wh/day)
3	128
4	170
5	255

A household with a need for 230Wh/day (the current needs for lighting, and in some cases a TV) will require just one panel when the radiation is 6kW/m²/d, and two panels when it is around 3kW/m²/d. This difference means an additional cost of some 30 to 40 per cent (the panels account for 30 to 40 per cent of the system cost) for the household located in the areas of least sunshine.

Solar thermal energy

There are many applications for the direct use of solar thermal energy: space heating and cooling, water heating, crop drying and solar cooking. It is a technology that is well understood and widely used in many countries throughout the world. Most solar thermal technologies have been in existence in one form or another for centuries, and have a well established manufacturing base in most sun-rich developed countries.

The most common use for solar thermal technology is for domestic water heating. Hundreds of thousands of domestic hot water systems are in use throughout the world, especially in areas such as the Mediterranean and Australia where there are large amounts of sunshine. It is a technology that is rapidly gaining acceptance as an energy saving measure in both domestic and commercial water heating applications. Presently, domestic water heaters are usually only found among wealthier sections of society.

Other technologies exist which take advantage of the free energy provided by the sun. Water heating technologies are usually referred to as *active solar* technologies, whereas other technologies, such as space heating or cooling, which passively absorb the energy of the sun and have no moving components, are referred to as *passive solar* technologies.

Technical

The nature and availability of solar radiation

Glass is transparent to short wave radiation but opaque to long wave, or heat, radiation. For storage of this trapped heat, a liquid or solid with a high thermal mass is employed. In a water heating system, water is the fluid that runs through the collector, whereas in a building the walls will act as the thermal mass. Pools or lakes are sometimes used for seasonal storage of heat.

If solar energy is being used to heat water by means of a collector panel, then the tilt and orientation of this panel is critical to the level of solar gain and hence the increase in temperature of the water. The collector surface should be oriented toward the sun as much as possible.

Solar thermal energy applications

Water heating. Low temperature (below 100°C) water heating is required in most countries of the world for both domestic and commercial use. There is a wide variety of solar water heaters available. The simplest is a piece of black plastic pipe, filled with water, and laid in the sun for the water to heat up. Simple solar water heaters usually comprise a series of pipes that are painted black, sitting inside an insulated box fronted with a glass panel, known as a 'solar collector'. The fluid to be heated passes through the collector and into a tank for storage. The fluid can be cycled through the tank several times to raise the temperature of the fluid to the required value. There are two common simple configurations for such a system, and they are outlined below.

○ The *thermosyphon* system makes use of the natural tendency of hot water to rise above cold water. The tank in such a system is always placed above the top of the collector and as water is heated in the collector it rises and is replaced by cold water from the bottom of the tank. This cycle will continue until the temperature of the water in the tank is equal to that of the panel. A one-way valve is usually fitted in the system to prevent the reverse occurring at night when the temperature drops. As hot water is drawn off for use, fresh cold water is fed into the system from the mains. As most solar collectors are fitted on the roofs of houses, this system is not always convenient, as it is difficult to site the tank above the collector, in which case the system will need a pump to circulate the water.

○ Pumped solar water heaters use a pumping device to drive the water through the collector. The advantage of this system is that the storage tank can be sited below the collector. The disadvantage, of course, is that electricity is required to drive the pump. Often the fluid circulating in the collector will be treated with an anti-corrosive and/or anti-freeze chemical. In this case a heat exchanger is required to transfer the heat to the consumer's hot water supply.

Integrated systems combine the functions of tank and collector to reduce cost and size.

Collector technology has made great advances in recent years. State-of-the-art collectors are manufactured from a variety of modern materials and are designed for optimal efficiency. Evacuated tube collectors have the heat-absorbing element placed within an evacuated glass sheath to minimize losses. System complexity also varies, depending on use. For commercial applications, banks of collectors are used to provide larger quantities of hot water as required. Many such systems are in use at hospitals in remote areas.

Solar cooking.   Solar cooking is a technology that has received a lot of attention in recent years. The basic design is that of a box with a glass cover. The box is lined with insulation, and a reflective surface is applied to concentrate the heat onto the pots. The pots can be painted black to help with heat absorption. The solar radiation raises the temperature sufficiently to boil the contents in the pots. Cooking time is often a lot longer than conventional cooking stoves, but there is no fuel cost.

Many variations have been developed on this theme but the main restriction has been one of reducing costs sufficiently to permit widespread dissemination. The cooker also has limitations in terms of being effective only during hours of strong sunlight. Another cooking stove is usually required for the periods when there is cloud or during the morning and evening hours. There have been extensive subsidized solar cooking stove dissemination programmes in India, Pakistan and China.

Crop drying.   Controlled drying is required for various crops and products, such as grain, coffee, tobacco, fruits and vegetables, herbs and spices, and fish. Their quality can be enhanced if the drying is carried out properly. Solar thermal technology can be used to assist with the drying of such products. Solar drying requires investment in equipment and structures, and often the cost of this hardware can be justified only for higher value products which require careful drying for their preservation. The main principle of operation is to raise the temperature of the product, which is usually held within a compartment or box, while at the same time passing air through the compartment to remove moisture. The flow of air is often promoted using the 'stack' effect, which takes advantage of the fact that hot air rises and can therefore be drawn upwards through a chimney, while drawing in cooler air from below. Alternatively, a fan can be used. The size and shape of the compartment varies depending on the product and the scale of the drying system. Large systems can use large barns, while smaller systems may have a few trays in a small wooden housing.

Solar crop drying technologies can help prevent depleting an area of fuelwood caused by the use of fuelwood or fossil fuels for crop drying (e.g. tobacco) and can also help to reduce the costs associated with these fuels and hence the cost of the product. Helping to improve and protect crops also has beneficial effects on health and nutrition.

Space heating. In colder areas of the world (including high-altitude areas within the tropics) space heating is often required during the winter months. Vast quantities of energy can be used to achieve this. If buildings are carefully designed to take full advantage of the sunshine that they receive then much of the heating requirement can be met by solar gain alone. By incorporating certain simple design principles, a new dwelling can be made to be fuel efficient and comfortable for habitation. The bulk of these technologies are architecture-based and passive in nature. The use of building materials with a high thermal mass (which stores heat), good insulation and large glazed areas can increase a building's capacity to capture and store heat from the sun. Many technologies exist to assist with diurnal heating needs but seasonal storage is more difficult and costly.

Space cooling. Countries within the tropics have little need for space heating. There is a demand, however, for space cooling. The majority of the world's warm-climate cultures have again developed traditional, simple, elegant techniques for cooling their dwellings, often using effects promoted by passive solar phenomena.

There are many methods of minimizing heat gain. These include siting a building in shade or near water, using vegetation or landscaping to direct wind into the building, and planning to optimize the prevailing wind and available shade. Buildings can be designed for a given climate – domed roofs and thermally massive structures in hot arid climates, shuttered and shaded windows to prevent heat gain, open structure bamboo housing in warm, humid areas. In some countries dwellings are constructed underground and take advantage of the relatively low and stable temperature of the surrounding ground. There are as many options as there are people.

Other uses. There are many other uses for solar thermal technology. These include refrigeration, air conditioning, solar stills and desalination of salt water, and electricity generation. Much effort has gone into the design of solar thermal power stations, which use solar radiation to raise steam for turbines to drive electric generators, but they are not relevant for rural energy applications at present. More information on these technologies is available in the relevant texts given in References and Resources.

Other issues

Manufacturing in remote areas
Many of the active solar technologies rely on sophisticated, exotic modern materials for their manufacture. This presents problems in countries where such materials have to be imported. Some countries do have a manufacturing base for

solar thermal products but it is often small, and by no means widespread throughout the world. The market for solar products, such as solar water heaters, is small and growing only slowly.

Solar passive technology, especially solar cooling, has traditionally been used in some countries. Many technological advances have been made in the design of 'solar buildings' during the last two decades, but again the level of technology is often high and expensive and out of reach of rural communities.

Dissemination

Solar cookers

Various attempts have been made to introduce solar cookers in Kenya. However, there have been major problems with the acceptability of this type of cooking. Of the people interviewed in a review survey, 90 per cent found the cooker to be too slow. Fifty-four per cent complained that it could not cook their preferred dishes, and in many cases the cooker could not cook enough for all the family members. In some areas where the solar box cooker is promoted there is a real scarcity of food and people will not experiment with the little food that they have. The cooker is seen as a very expensive item by over 53 per cent of the respondents, especially since it can cook only during the day.

Socio-economic factors influence adoption more than the technical features of the cooker. The survey showed that the way the stove is promoted is a major factor. If these stoves are to be used widely, then a more sensitive way of promoting them will be needed, and the problems listed above will have to be addressed.

Source: Personal communication Stephen Gitonga, Intermediate Technology, Kenya

6

Key technology issues

Grid versus stand-alone electrical generation and supply

In many countries, rural electrification statistics show that less than 25 per cent of rural households have access to electricity. The reasons for this are mainly the large distances over which the electricity has to be transmitted, and the dispersed nature of the population in rural areas. As a result, the costs of rural electrification are very high, plus there are technical difficulties in constructing and maintaining the extension lines. Even where the numbers of village connections are high, often there are only one or two households connected in each village. This is because the majority of households cannot afford a connection.

There are some locations where a decision between grid connection and decentralized generation must be made

Photograph: Intermediate Technology

The alternative to grid electricity supply is a decentralized power plant that supplies electricity directly to an isolated community. Such 'stand-alone' plants can provide electrical power to the most remote communities, which have almost no chance of grid connection. In addition, where such schemes are owned by the community, it may mean that the uptake of electricity connection by community members is relatively high.

There are some locations where a decision between grid connection and decentralized generation will have to be made. This chapter explains some of the technical, economic and managerial issues that will influence which type of electrical supply system is most suited to a village.

Technical and loading characteristics
When choosing a power supply system for a rural community there are several technical factors and loading characteristics that have to be considered.

Distance from the existing grid
If the community to be connected is a very long way from the existing grid, then there will have to be consideration of whether the cost of extending the grid is justified in either economic or social terms. There is often a cut-off distance at which grid extension is not viable. Also, the terrain between the grid and the village must be considered to see if there are difficulties, such as mountains or marshes, which can make line extension very difficult. For example, much of Nepal's rural population lives in dispersed villages or farms in the Himalayan mountains where landslides are a common feature. The practicalities of grid extension are extremely difficult in these circumstances. It is in such locations, far from the grid, where stand-alone systems are most effective.

Load density
The density of the load is the quantity of power demanded in a specified area. If there is a high electricity demand in a small area, then there will be a strong

Load density can affect the viability of stand-alone power plants
Photograph: Intermediate Technology/Andrew Barnett

justification for a grid connection in that area. However, most rural communities will require small quantities supplied to dispersed households, resulting in very low load densities. Low load density will also affect the viability of some stand-alone power plants.

Where loads are very dispersed, it may be more practical to consider supplying household systems, such as photovoltaic systems, rather than community systems that may require extensive distribution systems. Alternatively, a central battery charging system may be an alternative to distributing power to individual house-holds. This is the case at the Nyafaru micro-hydro system in the Zimbabwe Eastern Highlands. This scheme supplies the immediate community with elec-tricity to their houses, but also provides a battery charging system for more remote farms in the area.

System power losses
A feature of many rural electrification systems is the significant power loss in the transmission and distribution system. This is particularly the case where lower voltage transmission lines, say 11kVA or 33kVA, are extended over very long distances. Power losses of over 20 per cent are not uncommon in rural systems. As in urban areas, theft of electricity may also be a problem. This results in:

o costly power supply
o poor service to rural communities due to frequent load shedding, and
o instability in the power supply, with fluctuating voltage and frequency, at the end of long rural transmission lines.

Grid extension to rural areas often involves not only longer lines, but also upgrading the transmission system to reduce losses. There comes a point at which the decision has to be made as to whether power lines should be extended, with risk of higher system losses, or whether a decentralized scheme can better serve the remote community (see the Hills District case study opposite).

Base load/peak load – demand-side management
Another limit of electricity grids in many countries is the level of power available to the grid: often there is a higher national demand for electricity than the grid can supply. Even national grids that can supply the base-load needs of the country, (assuming all its power plants are fully functional), sometimes experi-ence difficulties in supplying the peak demand for power. Priority is usually given to industry and the larger cities. This will result in rural communities having a poor quality power supply, with frequent load shedding at peak hours. In many countries, the peak demand is for lighting and water heating in the evenings and early mornings. (See the load curve in Figure 6.1.)

Extending the rural electricity network without increasing the country's capa-city for power production can often further worsen the quality of the electricity service. Decentralized power production can help to alleviate the power supply problems for rural communities.

Many rural communities use electricity almost exclusively for lighting in the evening. This means that the revenue collected by the power companies from the

112

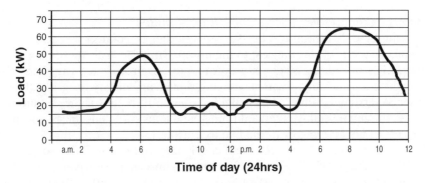

Figure 6.1: *Typical load curve for a rural area with some industrial load*

rural community will be very low. Using the available power for income-generating activities as well as lighting makes grid extension more financially viable. Stand-alone systems with a low load factor will not be economically sustainable. One advantage of community-owned stand-alone power systems is that the development of productive end uses for the power can be better planned into the development of the power system.

Case study of the Hill Districts of Uttar Pradesh, North India
The grid supply to the hill district of Chamoli is through a 33kVA transmission line which extends over 150km. The losses in the rural supply in Chamoli are over 30 per cent, with load shedding and voltage and frequency fluctuations common. The author had the experience in the district of reading one evening, as the incandescent light bulb in the room became dimmer and dimmer until it was necessary to supplement the light from the bulb with candlelight in order to continue reading. An alternative supply of power through micro-hydro power has been piloted in the area to supply rural communities.

One micro-hydro scheme, Dior, in the neighbouring district of Pauri, had been supplying electricity to a number of local villages. The villagers were provided with low-cost connections, and many people took a lighting load. The demand was not controlled, and the plant never operated to its design power output; as a result, more lighting loads have been connected than the system can supply. At the same time, no daytime connections had been taken in any of the villages. The outcome of this is that the powerhouse does not operate at all during the day, but there is not enough power to supply the evening load. The villages have been scheduled so that each village is given power only on agreed days of the week to limit the daily load on the plant. This scheme indicates where load management is vital for a decentralized scheme to be successful.

Source: A. Doig, 'Energy resources and the role of mini and micro hydro power in North India', PhD Thesis, University of Edinburgh, 1994

113

Economic criteria for grid or stand-alone supplies

The main factor affecting the decision of whether to connect a scheme to the national electricity grid is the cost to the utility. Rural electrification schemes are often heavily subsidized by the more profitable consumers – industry and urban customers. Alternatively, there may be a government subsidy for grid extension as a social service. Utilities will usually have a cut-off point for the distance that the grid line can be viably extended for a given number of consumers, which will be based mainly on the cost of the line extension.

For a stand-alone scheme, the main cost is the installation of the power plant itself plus the cost of distribution. Community-owned power plants may have either a low interest loan or a grant to cover a substantial part of the installation costs (see the section on Financing options in Chapter 2). Grants and subsidies available for various power supply options will influence the choice of options significantly.

Billing and tariff collection are a particular problem in rural areas, because of the dispersed nature of the population. Utilities have problems because the cost of reading meters and collecting tariffs can be higher than the revenue collected from rural communities who use electricity for lighting only. This is often the case when the revenue collector has to travel from a central office in town.

High revenue collection costs

Cost estimates for monthly meter reading, billing, collection and accounting expenses vary widely. For meter reading alone, per-customer costs in more populated rural areas range from $0.03 in Bangladesh and parts of Guatemala to $0.15 and more in Costa Rica and El Salvador. When bill preparation and serving charges and overheads are taken into account, the total cost of meter reading, billing and accounting is approximately three-and-a-half times the basic meter reading cost. Hence, the total cost ranges from $0.10 to more than $0.50 in more populated areas.

Revenue collection costs can be reduced by households with metered connection supplying electricity to nearby households, either legally or illegally. In Bangladesh such sub-connections are allowed and it is estimated that an average of 2.5 families are supplied by each meter. However, this can lead to exploitation of the sub-connected, usually the poorer households, by the metered consumer charging excessive amounts for the electricity supplied. This has been observed in Nepal.

There are a number of solutions that can specifically help low-income households to obtain electricity connection and help utilities to meet their required return on investment. These are: load limiters
prefabricated wiring systems
community involvement
tariff reforms

Extracted from: N. Smith, Affordable Electricity Installation for Low-income Households in Developing Countries, Intermediate Technology Consultants, Rugby, 1995

In the case of decentralized schemes, the community may be able to establish a means of payment better suited to their situation, for example payment at a local shop. Also, the tariff system need not be based on a meter reading, but on the capacity of power supplied to individual houses (usually regulated by circuit-breakers).

Ownership and management issues

Cost and technical constraints, however, are not the only factors that will influence the successful supply of power from either grid or stand-alone schemes. There are issues of ownership and management of the power supply system. With utility supply, the management is centralized, usually in the nearest cities or possibly in a district office. A stand-alone system will often have a decentralized ownership and management system, with either an entrepreneur running the plant as a commercial venture or the community running the village supply scheme. Some of the pros and cons of centralized versus decentralized ownership and management of power supply systems are given in Table 6.1.

Table 6.1: Pros and cons of centralized and decentralized ownership and management of rural power supply

For	Against
Centralized management of grid	
Financial risk on utility	No stake in power supply, so lack of interest in maintaining it
Management capacity already exists	Operation and maintenance staff often brought in from outside community
Technical capacity already exists	Bureaucratic management
	Repairs take longer because they must be approved by central management
	Tariff collection expensive
	No load management
	Disputes between utility and community possible
Decentralized management (community-owned stand-alone scheme)	
Interests in continual operation of scheme	Financial risk placed on community
Load management possible	Technical training required
Flexible tariffs possible	Management training required
Repairs made quickly	Outside assistance required for major repairs (costly)
Less bureaucracy	Local disputes possible if management breaks down
Local person employed as operator	
Local people provide labour, reducing initial capital required for scheme	

Cost comparison of energy options

This section gives some examples of the current cost of various energy technologies. It starts with some issues that must be considered when making a comparison of technologies. The next section gives some general indicators and trends of the current cost comparisons of energy technologies, as given in recent literature. The section on Financial performance in Chapter 2 describes methods used for making cost comparisons of particular technologies in site-specific conditions.

Issues to consider

The comparison of energy options is not simply the comparison of the cost of producing one unit of energy from the different sources. There are a number of factors that have to be considered when comparing the costs of energy production.

Time value of money

There are some energy sources that have high capital but low running costs (which is often the case for renewable energy sources), whereas there are others that have low capital cost but high running costs (such as some fossil fuel options). In order to make a full comparison of financial performance, it is essential to make a more detailed financial analysis, which considers the change in the value of money over time (see the section on Financial performance).

Energy services

It is essential to compare like with like. It is not useful to compare cooking fuel costs with electric lighting costs, but it is possible to compare the cost of electric cooking with biomass cooking costs. The comparison should not be with particular energy technologies, but with the cost of those technologies supplying a particular energy service (see the section on Energy service requirements), such as cooking, lighting, battery charging, mechanical power or water pumping. For example, the case of refrigeration, presented in the next section, demonstrates cost comparisons based on the use of solar energy and gas for refrigeration.

Local manufacturing or imported technology

The cost of an energy technology in a country will depend on whether the technology was produced locally or imported. Often, if the skills to produce the equipment are available, the cost of producing and installing the technology is substantially reduced. Maintenance costs will also be less, as there is no need to bring in outside expertise to repair the equipment.

Hidden subsidies

Comparing the real cost of energy technologies can be particularly difficult if there are direct or indirect subsidies for particular energy sources. For example, many countries subsidize rural grid electricity supplies and kerosene (see the section on Financing options). This will sometimes bias the cost comparison against those technologies that have no subsidy.

116

Table 6.2: Options for meeting energy service requirements

Energy option	Energy service requirement			
	Cooking and heating	Lighting	Mechanical: workshops, mills, pumps	Television and radio
Human power			✓	
Biomass	✓	✓		
Biogas	✓	✓		
Electric grid	✓	✓	✓	✓
Diesel/petrol	✓	✓	✓	✓
Kerosene	✓	✓		
Charcoal	✓			
Mini/micro-hydro	✓	✓	✓	✓
Photovoltaics		✓		✓
Wind power		✓	✓	✓
Solar passive	✓			
Candles		✓		

'No cost' fuels
One particular difficulty is comparing the cost of fuels that have a commercial value with fuels that have, effectively, no cost. For example, most rural house-holds will use fuelwood collected from common grounds. It must be noted that the time taken to collect wood could otherwise be used for productive means in the household if the wood is replaced by a commercial fuel. Also, there may be social value in reducing the time required for fuel collection. (The time freed could be used to give more effective childcare, or for rest, for example.) Similarly, there may be local environmental gains in changing from a 'no cost' fuel, for example, if there is a fuelwood scarcity in the local area. There are other social issues which must be considered, such as the disempowerment of women resulting from changes in their household role.

Cost comparisons
This section looks at some figures of cost comparison from recent literature, as a guide to the estimated cost of various energy forms. It must be noted that the actual cost of technologies can be very site specific, so the costs given below should be regarded as indicative, not definitive.

Electricity production
Cost comparisons of five rural electrification options are given in Table 6.3. This shows that the cost of grid electricity can be very expensive in remote locations or where populations are dispersed. Installation costs in Kenya can be more than 120 000 KSh, more than the cost of installing a photovoltaic system. The running costs of PV and grid supplies are similar. While diesel is the cheapest option for installation, it has the highest running costs.

Table 6.3: Comparison of typical costs for electricity supply types in rural Africa

Electricity supply type	Cost (US$/kWh)
Grid (Line extension for 3km for 50 families)	0.30
Grid (Line extension for 1km for 50 families)	0.17
Diesel Generator (50 families receiving 25kWh/ month)	0.50
Micro-hydro (At capital cost of US$1500/kW capacity)	0.15
Solar PV	0.25

Source: *Rural Energy and Development: Improving Energy Supplies for Two Billion People*, World Bank, Washington, 1996

Lighting

Figure 6.2 shows that a fluorescent lamp will be more than 40 times more effective at providing light than a kerosene lamp. This indicates that the quality of service is a key factor when comparing choices for lighting options. While candles, say, may be a cheap option, the energy service they provide is far inferior to electric lighting.

Tables 6.4 and 6.5 compare the lifetime costs of domestic lighting from a kerosene hurricane lamp and a PV lantern. This example assumes a

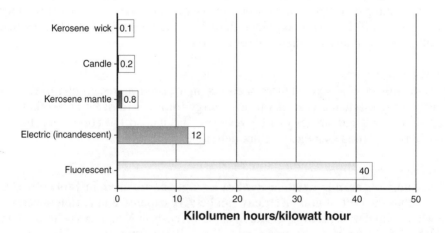

Figure 6.2: *Energy efficiency and lighting*

Lighting options must suit local circumstances

Photograph: Intermediate Technology/Lindel Caine

discount factor of 10 per cent. In this case the PV light kit works out to be the most cost-effective over the lifetime, though the initial cost of the PV light kit is much higher. However, the result for PV is very sensitive to the discount factor used (see the section on Financing options).

Cooking

Comparison of prices for cooking in an urban area in India show that, although the unit price of LPG is much higher, on the basis of price per useful energy output it is the cheapest option. The drawback of LPG cooking is the cost of the stove itself, which can be prohibitively high to very poor households.

Table 6.4: Data for domestic lighting life cycle cost comparison

General data

Analysis period	12 years
Discount rate	10%
Lighting demand	4h/day

Hurricane lamp data (per lamp)

Capital cost	US$8
Life	3 years
Fuel consumption	0.03 l/hour
Fuel price	US$/l 0.8
Light output	50 lm

PV lighting kit data

Capital cost	US$350
Light output (per lamp)	400 lm

The kit comprises

Item	Replacement cost (US$)	Life (years)
PV module 18Wp	0	12
Battery 70Ah	70	3
Tubes (2 × 8W)	8	3
Regulator	100	6

Source: J-P. Louineau et al., *Rural Lighting*, IT Publications, London, 1994

119

Table 6.5: Direct cost comparison of lighting output

Flame-based household lighting		PV lighting kit	
Cost per hour of lighting	$0.07/hour	Cost per hour of lighting	$0.06/hour
Lumen output	100 lumen	Lumen output	800 lumen
Cost per light output	$0.66/klm-hour	Cost per light output	$0.07/klm-hour

(1klm =1000lm)

Cooking with wood in urban areas is the most expensive option. This is unlikely to be the case in rural areas, as wood is often collected free. However, this does not reflect the lost opportunity cost of using the time spent collecting fuelwood for more economically productive activities.

Refrigeration for vaccine storage in remote locations
Vaccine storage requires a very high quality service from the energy source. It is essential that the refrigerator is constantly operational. Therefore, the energy supply should be constant. Table 6.6 shows a comparison of refrigeration powered by photovoltaic cells via a battery and by gas. The first columns shows the lifetime costs of the two options without considering the time value of money. This shows that the PV option is more expensive in terms of capital cost. The choice will therefore depend on the availability of gas – if gas is not available, or is very uncertain, then PV will be the best or only choice. The last two columns indicate the annualized costs, considering the time value of money. This time uses a discount factor of 14 per cent. (At this discount factor the PV system is still the more costly option.)

Table 6.6: Comparison of refrigeration powered by PV and by gas

	Cost		Annualized costs with discount factor	
	PV US$	Gas US$	PV US$	Gas US$
Investment				
Total investment	5050	1000	1135	140
Running costs				
Gas (1bottle/wk)		260		260
Maintenance/yr	50	30	50	30
Total annual cost (discounted)			1185	430

Discount value: 14%
Source: WHO, *Vaccine refrigerator: lessons learned from large-scale programme survey, Geneva, 1991*. (Annualized costs calculated by the authors)

A consideration that the cost comparison does not show is the reliability of the power source. Both options have good records in terms of efficiency and standards. However, if gas shortages are expected over a long period (more than three months) the solar option might be considered. It could be possible to have, say, a year's stock of gas available in case of a shortage, but this would raise the initial investment by US$780. For the case of the solar-powered refrigerator, there must be a guaranteed sunshine availability or there must be sufficient battery storage available to cover days when the sun is not shining. Gas is a realistic option only if it is readily available at an affordable price.

PART III

CASE STUDIES

1. THE CHALAN MICRO-HYDRO SCHEME (PERU)

Location

Chalan is located in the northern Department of Cajamarca in the Andes of Peru at an altitude of 2750 metres above sea level. The village lies at the head of a deep valley which falls steeply to the River Marañon, a tributary of the Amazon. Chalan was established by a Spanish settler during the colonial period in an area far from the main trading routes in the Andes. The development of the village has been very slow, with the main advances taking place during the 1980s and 1990s. The road from Celendon was extended to Chalan in 1985 and a radio link to the national telephone system was established recently. The village now has a basic health centre and school, and three years ago the village council purchased a goods vehicle for general work in the area.

Population

Chalan is the main settlement in the District of Miguel Iglesias and has a population of 540 people in 120 families. There are 19 other small settlements or hamlets in the surrounding area, all of which use Chalan as their main centre. The nearest large town is Celendon, which is eight hours away on horseback.

Many of the families who live in Chalan gain a cash income by working as labourers for landowners along the banks of the Marañon. The descent of 2000 metres takes eight hours on foot and the villagers generally leave Chalan at the beginning of the week and return with tropical fruit and vegetables grown under the different climatic conditions in time for the Sunday market. Almost all families in the area are engaged in agricultural work on their own smallholdings as their main occupation. The average annual income per household is $400.

The micro-hydro scheme

Chalan lies around 80km from the nearest transmission line of the electricity grid, a journey which takes seven hours by vehicle due to the poor state of the road. The initiative for the micro-hydro scheme came from the mayor and an NGO called DIACONIA, which was assisting local farmers with irrigation and other agricultural technologies. An approach was made to Intermediate Technology's Energy Programme in Cajamarca and a process of planning was begun.

The funding for the scheme came from four sources; a loan from the credit programme run by Intermediate Technology, a donation from DIACONIA, from the village council, and the labour of every family in Chalan, who agreed to contribute a set amount of time in constructing the channel, installing the pipe and building the powerhouse. A total of 4318 person days of labour were provided by the community. Intermediate Technology Peru provided supervision throughout the construction of the scheme and provided technical and management support and training during the first year of operation.

The capital cost of the project was $43 000, providing direct connections for 80 families to date, with most of the remaining households expected to connect in

Chalan village communication system – powered by the village micro-hydro scheme

Photograph: Intermediate Technology/Steve Fisher

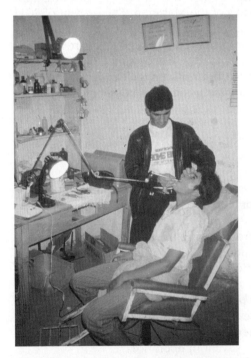

Chalan's dentist is micro-hydro powered

Photograph: Intermediate Technology/Steve Fisher

the future. The average tariff is 6 soles ($2) per month. A further 617 families are indirect beneficiaries of the scheme, making use of improved health, education, battery-charging, agro-processing, workshop and communication services, as well as public lighting in the village.

The Chalan Micro-hydro Scheme is managed by an elected committee, which is independent of the village council and takes particular responsibility for operation and maintenance, collecting tariffs, promoting safe and efficient use of the energy and managing the introduction of new uses such as workshop equipment. The scheme employs two full-time operators and a part-time administrator and is in operation every day of the year between the hours of 12 noon and 12 midnight.

The technical details of the project are as follows:

Channel	Length 830 metres
	Slope 4 in 1000
	Design flow 52 litres/second
	Concrete-lined
Penstock	Head 96 metres
(pressure pipe)	Length 202 metres
	Diameter 20cm
	Material PVC Class 15, 10 and 7.5
Turbine	Vertical shaft Pelton with three jets
Generator	Nominal power 38kW (effective 25kW)
	Voltage 220 volts, three-phase
	Frequency 60 Hz
	Speed 1800 r.p.m.
	Regulation by electronic load controller
Distribution	Maximum voltage drop 5 per cent
	Public lighting, 30 streetlamps
	Domestic connections of between 50 and 350 watts per household

Update

As at June 1998, the Chalan micro-hydro scheme was operating well and providing the local community with a wide range of energy services. 87 households in the immediate community benefit directly from the scheme. Around 240 households benefit indirectly.

Streetlighting from the Chalan micro-hydro scheme

Photograph: Intermediate Technology/Steve Fisher

127

2. THE SCALE OF HYDRO POWER DEVELOPMENT
(Appropriate hydro in Nepal: The case of Arun III)

Nepal is one of the few countries in the world that could easily generate all the electricity it needs from hydro power. The government is well aware of this potential and has plans to develop Nepal's water resources. The initial plans have concentrated on large-scale schemes.

Nepal has a large hydro power resource
Photograph: Intermediate Technology/
Adam Harvey

In August 1995, the President of the World Bank, James Wolfensohn, suddenly cancelled the Bank's proposed $175 million loan to Nepal for the controversial Arun III hydroelectric project. Campaigning groups in Nepal, the UK and the USA see this as a major step towards an appropriate energy policy for Nepal.

This case study explains the reasons why the non-governmental organizations (NGOs) opposed the Arun project and describes the appropriate approach to hydro development that has been proposed as an alternative.

Why large dams?
Large dams can serve a number of purposes, other than the supply of hydro power. The reservoir created by the dam can be used for supplying water for drinking or for irrigating agricultural land. The flooded area may provide new fishing opportunities or be used for recreational purposes. In some places, large dams are used as a means of controlling annual floods downstream from the dam.

The World Bank, along with other inter-governmental institutions such as the Asian Development Bank, has been financing large dam construction over the past few decades, with all these benefits in mind. There has been a growing movement in opposition to such large developments, however, because of the damaging environmental impacts in the area affected by the dam. This considerable opposition has forced the World Bank to review its role as a promoter of large dam projects.

128

The history of the Arun project

The history of Arun III began in 1985 when a Japanese report identified the site as a potential 402MW hydro project. The World Bank got involved in 1987, when it selected Arun III as its preferred option for hydro development in Nepal. However, it was not until six years later that the potential donors for the Arun project met to produce a plan of action for developing 'Baby Arun', a smaller (though still large) project of 201MW plus a 122km access road to the site. The dam was to be constructed in the Arun valley which runs down from Tibet, close to Mount Everest, and was projected to be 155m wide and 85m high. The project was to cost about $1082 million – the equivalent of more than one-and-a-half times the Government of Nepal's annual development budget – a considerable debt burden.

It was at this point, in February 1993, that a public meeting was organized by local NGOs in the capital, Kathmandu, to discuss the development of Baby Arun. At this meeting the alternative approach to hydro development was proposed.

The issues at Arun

Arguments for Baby Arun

- Arun would produce maximum electricity output all year; other schemes do not produce as much electricity during the dry season
- The geological investigations proved it to be a favourable site
- The road to the Arun project site would also provide access for further hydro development in the area after Arun was built
- The Nepal government could gain an income from the project, which could be given to the social sector
- There is urgent need for additional electricity supplies
- Since Nepal is not capable of developing Arun, why not let outsiders build it?
- The World Bank loan was accompanied by a grant of $175 million.

Arguments against Baby Arun

- No other (smaller) projects would be built while Arun was under construction
- High risk of developing one big scheme instead of spreading risk over several smaller schemes
- The project was hugely expensive because technologies, finance and expertise were all to be brought in from outside
- It would be 10 years before any benefit would be felt
- The development of the local hydro power industry would be crushed
- Arun would do nothing to help the 85 per cent of the population without electricity to gain access to it
- The cost of power from Arun would increase the electricity cost to the Nepalese consumers
- It would create environmental and social damage far beyond Nepal's capacities for providing compensation
- Arun would cost $1082 million, one-and-a-half times Nepal's national annual development budget.

129

Environmental impacts and impact on local people

There are concerns about large dams because of the expected environmental impact of the flooding in the area behind the dam. There are concerns about the welfare of the people who will be moved out of the area to be flooded.

These have been the key issues behind the opposition to the huge dam projects at Narmada, which will flood over 1000 square kilometres of land, and the Three Gorges dams, which will relocate over 1 million people from the flooded area.

These were not the main issues with the Arun project. The area to be flooded at Arun was not great, and the number of people to be relocated was low. In fact, the main threat to the local area was the environmental impact of the road to be built to the dam site, which would cut through the sensitive countryside.

The local people in the valley were not in general opposed to the Arun project, as they thought it would boost the local economy, which is currently based on subsistence farming and portering. However, a World Bank study suggested an overall negative impact of the road, and it was unclear how the proposed mitigation measures would be implemented.

The key issues at Arun were more complex and related to the development capacity of Nepal, that is:

○ the investment costs
○ the impact on the Nepalese hydro industry, and
○ the impact on the energy sector in Nepal.

Local hydro power capacity

One of the strongest arguments against the project was that the Arun project would do nothing to build capacity of the growing Nepalese hydro power industry. Arun's size meant that it would have to be built entirely by international contractors, and local companies would have no significant role in it. This was a classic example of what is called 'tied aid': for example, the turbines were to come from Germany (the German government was one of the funders) and the transmission lines from Japan (another funder). In addition, the World Bank insisted that Arun take priority over other power generating schemes, meaning that the development of local industry and expertise would be stifled.

The basic elements for a self-sufficient hydro industry already exist in Nepal. There is engineering, research and manufacturing capacity available to build schemes up to 60MW. Training remains a huge need – most engineers still have to train outside the country.

Investment cost

By far the greatest concern, in financial terms, was the risk that the huge burden of debt, about $1 billion, that would be placed on the Nepalese government would not generate sufficient benefits. Although in global terms the dam is not a very large power project (Baby Arun would have been 201MW, compared to the Itaipu Dam in Brazil which supplies 12 600MW and the Three Gorges Dam in China which will eventually supply 18 200MW), Arun would have been the largest infrastructural project undertaken by the Nepalese government. Those opposed to the project believed that the risks of such a venture would far outweigh the gains. Using such a huge amount of public money on one project that would only come on line in 10 years, was worrying. The risk of putting 'all the eggs in one basket' applied to all risks, including: cost over-runs, technical problems, time over-runs, administrative delays and natural catastrophes such as flooding.

Energy and power development in Nepal

The Arun scheme would have provided a very reliable supply of power to the Nepalese national grid, which predominantly supplies power to the cities and more densely populated areas. However, 85 per cent of the Nepalese people do not have access to electricity at all. The majority of the population of Nepal live in rural areas, many in the remote hills and mountains of the Himalayas which dominate the country. Most have very little chance of ever being connected to the national grid system.

The electricity to be generated at Arun would have been transported out of the valley area by high-voltage lines to the urban plains of Nepal. Thus, the people most affected by the project would not reap the benefits.

Additional electricity was needed immediately, but Arun would take at least 10 years to construct. There was little mention in the project as to how the more immediate electricity needs would be met in the 10 years while Arun was being built.

Alternative hydro options

Nepal's need for additional power in the next 15 years will be in the region of 700MW to 1600MW depending on the growth of the economy. The alternative approach proposed for hydro power would allow hydro development at a steady rate, with a number of plants coming on-line each year.

Mini- and micro-hydro

With 85 per cent of Nepal's population living in rural areas far from the grid, mini- and micro-hydro offer many opportunities for providing a clean and developmentally sound source of power. Work has been carried out to develop micro-hydro in Nepal for the past two decades, particularly in remote rural villages where connection to the national grid will never be feasible. Over 1000 micro-hydros systems have been built in the past 25 years and more than one million people have use of mills powered by micro-hydro. While this does not substitute for grid electricity delivered to towns and larger industries, it does provide a basis for development of expertise in hydro power.

Medium- and small-scale hydro

It is not suggested that micro-hydro is a direct replacement for large-hydro, as micro-hydro cannot supply the increasing demands of the national grid. Medium-scale (15–100MW) and small-scale (1–15MW) will be required to feed electricity to the grid. Developing smaller schemes would not only lessen the risks and enable power to be produced earlier, but would reduce costs by enabling Nepalese companies to perform large parts of the work. There are nearly 80 possible hydro power schemes in the small and medium size range in Nepal that

131

Micro-hydro power scheme in Nepal

Photograph: Intermediate Technology/Adam Harvey

could be developed over the next few years. The largest of these is a 60MW system at Kankai. The 80 schemes have a total generating capacity of over 1200MW. Three-quarters of this power could be delivered by 29 medium-sized schemes. Since the cancellation of Arun, such schemes are being reconsidered for implementation by the private sector.

Hydro development fund
To achieve the goal of developing medium-, mini- and micro-scale projects, the NGOs (led by a Nepalese group called the Alliance for Energy) proposed that the finance offered for Arun should be redirected for the development of a number of smaller projects across the country. They proposed that a revolving investment fund of US$600 million be invested for the development of a range of hydro power schemes in the country. This fund should allow Nepal to become self-sufficient in hydro power generation and reduce the country's dependence on foreign aid and technical assistance in the long run.

The essential features of this approach are:

○ investing in building local technical capability
○ switching to a decentralized model of power production, which ensures a sharing of risks between a number of schemes, and
○ adopting an evolutionary approach to hydro power development which encourages the industry to move ahead in progressive stages, taking on larger projects as its capabilities grow and mature.

The outcome
The Arun project became a test case for the World Bank's new Independent Inspection Panel, which was set up to examine possible breaches of Bank policy,

132

where local people felt their lives would be affected adversely by a proposed project. On the eve of the publication of the panel's report, which was known to be critical of the Bank, President James Wolfensohn announced that the Bank would no longer consider backing the Arun project.

The cancellation of the loan for the 201MW Arun project in 1995 has forced the Nepalese government to reassess its hydro power strategy. The government has adopted a more diverse approach, giving greater support to smaller, capacity-building schemes, which use local engineers and manufacturers where possible.

Another result is that the World Bank has now supported the development of a Nepal Power Development Fund. This will be used to develop the small and medium hydro power projects in Nepal to meet domestic demand for electricity and to export power where possible. The hydro projects to be developed by the Fund will have to be accepted by a screening process, which will assess the technical and economic viability as well as the environmental and social impacts of the projects. The screening process will take account of the opinions of community groups affected by the projects.

Electric lighting makes productive work possible in the evenings

Photograph: Intermediate Technology/ Caroline Penn

Private development of the Arun project

It now looks possible that the Arun project may still be built by private companies and with private financing. If this goes ahead, it is likely that the electricity produced will be sold directly to India or China. Private sector investment will, however, remove the burden of finance and responsibility from the Nepalese government. The government will be free to develop other hydro power sector projects which are more favourable to Nepalese development needs.

The remaining concerns over the private development of Arun are the environmental and social effects. The private developers must ensure that the social and environmental impact of the dam, and the road to the dam, will be minimized.

3. RURAL STOVES IN WEST KENYA: PRODUCTION AND COMMERCIALIZATION

More than two-thirds of the population in Kenya rely on biomass (wood, charcoal, agricultural residues) for energy. The majority of biomass energy users are poor communities that are faced with problems associated with the continuous use of inefficient stoves. Although improved stoves are not the only means of addressing this, they play a crucial role in reducing fuel consumption and improving overall family health and safety in the kitchen.

Intermediate Technology's rural stoves project in West Kenya evolved from two earlier activities:

○ a project to field test woodburning stoves, and
○ a training project for women potters.

The woodburning stoves project tested a range of improved woodburning stove designs in a number of regions of Kenya, with a view to determining which was most suitable for widespread dissemination among rural households. The project gave clear indication that the one-pot improved ceramic stove (Mandeleo or Upesi) was widely acceptable among potential users.

The training project for women potters was designed to assist groups of potters in Nyanza province, Western Kenya, to improve the viability of their production activities by introducing new products to meet local demands.

The product

The Upesi stove goes through several stages before it is ready for installation in a kitchen. It is first fashioned from pottery clay, using a mould. It is then dried for two weeks before being fired in a kiln. The firing takes six hours.

The stoves are usually unloaded from the kiln one day after firing, when they are cold enough to be handled. The fired stoves can then be installed in the houses using a base of a mixture of mud and stones.

Depending on the skills of the installer, the installation takes between 15 minutes and two hours to carry out (if all the material is in place beforehand). After installation, the user has to allow the stove to dry for one week before using it.

When stoves are used correctly, they considerably reduce the levels of smoke emissions. A survey carried out in 1994 showed that in every situation Upesi stoves are cleaner than the traditional fireplace. However, it is important that users observe sound cooking practices, such as drying wood before use and cutting it into small pieces to burn more easily.

Working with the beneficiaries

The improved woodstove being promoted by ITDG in west Kenya is known as the 'Upesi'. (It was originally known as the 'Maendeleo' stove, because it was

Women making Upesi stoves

Photograph: Intermediate Technology/Tim Jones

Firing Upesi stoves

Photograph: Intermediate Technology/Neil Cooper

first promoted in Kenya by the Maendeleo Ya Wanawake organization, working in conjunction with the GTZ Special Energy Project (SEP).)

The project promoting the 'Upesi' focused on benefits to the producers and the development of a commercial market for stoves. The experience over the last three decades shows that commercial production and marketing is paramount in the creation of a sustainable business for stoves.

The project worked with women because pottery (and in particular stove production) is a task that is well suited to the needs of women in rural communities. In addition, there is a potential for social benefits such as increased recognition of women's status and greater control over household budgets.

Woman making an Upesi stove
Photograph: Intermediate Technology/Neil Cooper

The Group-Led Action Plan

The project provided training to 19 women's groups of potters in West Kenya (Nyanza, Western, and parts of Rift Valley provinces). Ten groups totalling 120 women have progressed to the extent where they have become recognized stove producers.

The project developed a participative approach (Group-Led Action Plan – GLAP) to ensure that the producer groups have controlled the extent of their involvement in the project and the nature and pace of their training. There is a series of steps designed to encourage and enable the stove producers to identify their needs and define the pace of the training that they receive from the project. There is no fixed timetable or pattern to the training. The aim is to ensure that only the most motivated and best organized groups continue with the training that is offered.

The project has encouraged the producer groups to participate in quarterly planning exercises at which the women are given the responsibility for defining their own training needs and devising the programmes. When this was first carried out, the targets set by the groups tended to be ambitious. Subsequent exercises have produced more realistic plans. The GLAP proved its effectiveness, especially with the new women's groups that executed all the GLAP-steps, and consequently appear to be more independent and self-confident compared to other groups.

Marketing

The initial market for the Upesi was developed during a period when similar stoves were partially subsidized by the Ministry of Agriculture through a GTZ fund. The continuation of this subsidy has led to artificially low prices and unequal competition. One of the key project targets, therefore, was to influence GTZ and the Ministry to accept a more realistic pricing structure which reflects the real costs of production.

Other steps were also necessary for the creation of a sustainable market.

○ It is essential that the improved product is reliable and affordable to rural people. In many cases of stove manufacture, the conditions needed to provide a quality product consistently have been overlooked, leading to a lack of confidence among customers. People with very little money need to know that what they are buying is reliable.
○ The availability of raw materials may be a major cause of failure. Pottery clay is the main raw material used in the manufacture of mud stoves. When producers are not within walking distance of their sources of clay, the cost of transporting the clay may make it too expensive.
○ A market, once created, can be damaged by low-cost and poor quality imitations.

This may have two major consequences.

○ Professional and long-established producers may not be able to compete with cheap imitations.
○ Consumers may go back to traditional stoves because of the poor quality. It may take time to rebuild consumer confidence. One solution is to certify and promote products that comply with certain quality criteria as shown in the following examples.

Example 1: Ceramic liner for KCJ, West Kenya

In West Kenya, an artisan introduced a three-month guarantee for the ceramic part of the Kenyan metal stove (KCJ: Kenya Ceramic Jiko)[1]. Currently, more than 10 000 improved stoves are produced each year. The bulk of the production is now controlled by the producers, retailers, and salesmen. The normal market has taken over from 'commercialization' carried out by the Ministry of Energy.

Example 2: Anagi stove, Sri Lanka

In Sri Lanka, households use ceramic stoves for cooking. An improved stove called the 'Anagi' was developed (in much the same way as the 'Upesi' in Kenya), in collaboration with Sri Lankan potters' groups.

A strategy for marketing and commercialization was also successfully implemented. Untrained producers started making cheap 'look-alike stoves' to imitate the 'Anagi' improved stove. The introduction of a label gave a quality assurance

---

[1] See Khennas, S., Walubengo, D. and Weyman, A. 'Rural stoves West Kenya evaluation', ITDG internal document, Nairobi, September 1995.

Stoves on sale in West Kenya showing 'Jiko' ceramic lining

Photograph: Intermediate Technology/ Jeremy Hartley

to customers who were keen to pay the full price.[2] The results are remarkable since, according to a recent evaluation, in the last six years some 450 000 Anagi improved woodburning stoves have been sold and the producers are making increased profits.

Economics

Overall, the project has achieved significant results. The annual production is over 12 000 Upesi stoves and 2500 liners for the Kenya Ceramic Jiko. The total profit[3] generated by the stoves' business could be estimated between 217 500 and 397 500Ksh for the women's groups.

Energy savings and the pay-back period. The pay-back period is a method largely used to measure the benefits for the consumer. The pay-back period is the time it takes for the cumulative measurable savings (firewood in this case) to equal the initial investment.

Anagi stove in use in Sri Lanka

Photograph: Intermediate Technology/Steve Bonnist

[2] For more details, see Ashley, C. and Young, P. 'Stoves for sale, practical hints for commercial dissemination of improved stoves', IDEA, FAO, IT, FWD, 1993.
[3] The profit may be estimated at 30KSh per UPESI and 15KSh per KCJ.

In this case, the Upesi selling price to the final consumer ranges between 100 and 120Ksh, that is an average selling price of 110Ksh. If the liner is installed, the consumer is generally charged 40Ksh on average, that is a mean of 150 Ksh[4]. The firewood savings[5] are estimated at 30 per cent when an Upesi stove replaces a three-stone fire, which is widely used in rural areas.[6]

Given an average rural family of six people and a consumption of 1.5kg per head, the daily firewood savings per household equipped with the Upesi stove are:

$$6 \times 1.5 \times 30\% = 2.7\text{kg}$$

Firewood pricing.   Firewood is rapidly becoming a market commodity in Western Kenya. The prices vary from district to district. Generally, firewood for domestic uses (cooking) is bought in bundles weighing 20kg and costing 20Ksh. The daily savings are therefore 2.7Ksh. The pay-back period is:

> without installation costs: 110:2.7 = 41 days
> with installation costs: 150:2.7 = 56 days

These figures mean that within a period of between one-and-a-half and two months, according to the options, the initial investment of the consumer is paid back by the total fuel savings over these respective periods. We can conclude that purchasing an Upesi stove is good value for the consumer, even when installation is paid for, since its life span exceeds three years. This pay-back period is likely to decline in the future as firewood prices rise in real terms.

Although these aggregate figures do not reflect the specific situation of each group, they give a good idea of the income and profits generated by this activity. It is, however, interesting to look at the economics of specific cases, such as that of the Webolela Women's Group.

Webolela Women's Group
Originally this group comprised 48 members. Currently, the active group is limited to 14 members, two of whom produce pots only. The capacity of the kiln is 65 Upesi and 35 KCJ liners.

To find out how labour or capital intensive this activity is, the different costs have been classified under the following main categories : raw material, labour and capital cost.

The wholesale price of the Upesi is 55Ksh, so the profit margin is 31Ksh. This represents a profit margin for the Upesi of 129 per cent. The cost of production of the KCJ liner is estimated to be 8Ksh. With a wholesale price of

---

[4] The mean is the average value. The mean for the installed UPESI is calculated according to the following formula: [(100+40)+(120+40)]/2 = 150.

[5] Up to 50 per cent were recorded in some cases. Our assumption of 30 per cent is based on savings observed in the field.

[6] Depending on the region, 80 to 99 per cent of the households cook with the three-stone fire, see GTZ, 'Micro- and macro-economic benefits of household energy conservation in rural areas of Kenya', July 1994, in-house publication.

Table 7.1: Production costs of the Webolela Women's Group (in Kenya shillings – Ksh)

Product	Unit	Price Ksh	Per stove Ksh
Water	1 drum for 30 stoves	60	2
Clay	Collection for 30 stoves	70	2.33
Clay preparation	7 days for 40Ksh for 30 stoves	280	9.33
Moulding	3 stoves per hour	7	2.3
Firewood			3
Loading	3 hours for 100 stoves	21	0.21
Firing	12 hours for 100 stoves	84	0.84
Off-loading	1.5 hours for 100 stoves	10.5	0.01
Storage	One hour	7	0.07
Capital cost	per stove	2	2
Losses (4%)*			0.76
Overhead			2
Total			24.94

Losses recorded by the project

Production cost = 24.9KSh

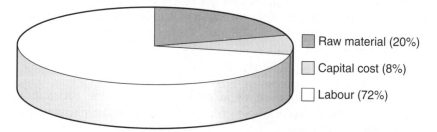

Raw material (20%)

Capital cost (8%)

Labour (72%)

Figure 7.1: *Production cost breakdown for the Upesi stove*

20Ksh, the profit margin per stove comes to 12Ksh (i.e. 150 per cent), which is particularly high.

In 1994, the Upesi production recorded by the project was 2038 stoves. This represents a profit of 67 250Ksh or 5605Ksh per capita. The KCJ production is not recorded by the project but is easily estimated. Sixty-five Upesi stoves and 35 KCJ liners are fired in a kiln at the same time, i.e. there is a ratio between the number of KCJ liners to Upesi stoves of 0.54. KCJ production was therefore 1100 units in 1994. This yielded a profit of 14 265Ksh for the group.

The total average profit generated by the stove production is 81 515Ksh or 6790Ksh per capita. Even if we assume that only 80 per cent of the production is actually sold, this figure is higher than the average income (e.g. employees on farms) in rural areas. It is worth noting that women have an additional income from other activities, mainly agriculture.

Lessons learned

- Participatory approaches need to be given time to work effectively.
- Technical training alone is insufficient. It needs to be accompanied by training in group organization, management, marketing and business skills.
- Working with women's groups can be a very effective way of reaching rural women. Group work tends to add to motivation and sustainability and ensures some distribution of benefits within the group.
- The selling of stoves can be a profitable business if measures are taken to ensure that the production of good quality stoves is maintained. A key lesson is that although dissemination strategies may vary, the normal mechanisms of the market should prevail. Income generation for all the players is essential for expansion of the market and in making the commercial production of stoves viable.
- The shorter the link between the producer and the final customers, the lower the prices. However, a shop-owner will rarely buy from a manufacturer but from a salesman or stockist who generally has a higher income to buy in bulk from the producer and sell to the retailer.
- The whole process before the commercialization phase is reached may span several years.

4. PHOTOVOLTAIC POWER FOR DOMESTIC AND INSTITUTIONAL END USES

The PV market comprises two different types of consumers:

○ institutions or small businesses such as schools or clinics, and
○ households.

PV can be used to supply small loads, such as water pumping
Photograph: Intermediate Technology/Smail Khennas

Indonesia household energy systems

A multilateral scheme
It is estimated that more than 20 million households in rural areas, totalling a population of about 110 million, do not have access to electricity. Since the beginning of the 1980s, Indonesia has developed a strategy aimed at increasing solar photovoltaic use in rural electrification programmes. The amount of sunshine is relatively high, with average figures of 4.5 to 5kWh/m²/day. So far, solar photovoltaic energy is supplying some 25 000 households with electricity and the installed capacity is estimated to be of 3MWp. Apart from lighting, which is the main market, PV is used for water pumping, refrigeration and communications. Recently, the Government of Indonesia has secured significant funds from the World Bank and the Global Environmental Facility (GEF) to provide lighting and

142

other electricity services to approximately 200 000 households. The total cost of the project is US$118 million of which 38 per cent is covered by the World Bank (US$20 million) and a GEF grant (US$24.3 million). Solar dealers (distributors) and end users are providing around 57 per cent of the project funding, a substantial contribution. The government is making a subsidy of a mere 1 per cent, the rest of the funding being sourced from commercial banks.

Loans are provided to the distributors on a commercial basis. Although the conditions attached to these loans are not easy to fulfil, the compliance to some extent with commercial rates is an important step towards the sustainability of the project. Currently credits granted on a commercial basis have a 24 per cent interest rate, a 48-month pay-back and 100 per cent collateralization.

Strategy for reaching rural households: example of Sudimara

Sudimara Energi Surya is a private company in Indonesia involved in the business of solar home systems for rural households. To reach rural customers, the company has set up a network of service centres responsible for sales, service and credit. This formula has the advantage of combining the key components of a project which are usually spread among various players. The service centres are also handling after-sales service to ensure that services are provided according to the standards, and to gather information. This network is operating at a sub-district level which comprises 5000 to 15 000 households. According to the company, some 200 to 300 customers can be reached each year within the sub-district. Solar generators come with a one-year guarantee, whereas the output is guaranteed for ten years.

Apart from the solar panels, which are imported, the company manufactures some key components and assembles the systems in its facilities located in Sukabami, West Java. For example, the solar regulator, the ballasts for the fluorescent lamps and the low wattage non-fluorescent bulbs are produced by Sudimara. In addition, the company follows the guarantee clauses for the components provided by other suppliers such as batteries and bulbs.

The mechanisms

Systems sold by the company include one to three panels, a battery, the cables and six very low wattage fluorescent lamps (3 watts and 2 watts). Apart from lighting, the system provides enough energy to supply a black and white TV and a tape recorder. Between October 1993 when the company started the commercialization and the end of 1995, more than 8000 panels were sold. The bulk of the systems are sold on credit, with a full rate of recovery so far. Although down-payments are relatively high (30 per cent of the costs), the market has grown steadily and it is likely that smaller down-payments will increase the sales dramatically. Such an option is not without financial risks, however.

PV for institutional end uses in Zimbabwe

Generally speaking, parastatal enterprises (national railways, army, schools, clinics) account for a large proportion of the market for PV in Zimbabwe. A survey carried out in 1991 shows that this sector accounts for more than 50 per

Table 7.2: Methods of payment for each system

	Cash ('000s Rp)	Credit ('000s Rp)
System with one panel	890	Down payment and 26 monthly instalments of 31/month
		Down payment and 31 monthly instalments of 26/month
System with two panels	1490	Down payment and 26 monthly instalments of 41.5/month
System with three panels	2190	Down payment and 26 monthly instalments of 62/month

Prices end 1995
Exchange rate September 1995: 1000Rp = US$0.45. In 1997, the local currency has been sharply depreciated due to the economic and financial crisis

cent of the installed capacity, which was 151kW. Because of their impact on education and health, it is interesting to analyse the systems installed in schools and clinics.

End uses
The survey was carried out in seven schools and 16 hospitals and clinics. It appears that the main end use is lighting (74 per cent) mainly for study or to light the wards. The other end uses are telecommunications and refrigeration.

Manufacturing
In Zimbabwe, at the beginning of the 1990s, some 10 manufacturers were involved in the solar PV system, although they were also engaged in the manufacturing of other products not related to PV. Batteries, control electronics, and light fittings are the main components produced by solar companies in Zimbabwe. One company, which installed most of the systems in the institutional sector, has its own facilities to assemble PV systems. The plant was supplied under a Canadian aid scheme and was designed to produce panels of 15Wp, 30Wp and 50Wp with a total installed capacity of 320kW/y. This capacity was not fully employed, mainly because of the lack of some components rather than the insufficient level of demand.

Maintenance
As far as schools are concerned, a community resident was responsible for the maintenance, but there was no checklist of tasks to carry out a proper maintenance. The only tasks were limited to adding distilled water to batteries and cleaning the terminals. Two-thirds of the failures were due to batteries and one-quarter to the bulbs (27 per cent). It was noticed that the quality of the maintenance was linked to the general management of the institution. With respect to

the size, small systems performed better than larger ones. There was not a great deal of difference in the maintenance between the systems that were donated and those paid for by the school.

Financing
On average, the systems had a size of 200Wp. Most of the systems were bought for cash, paid by either the donors or the institution. School fees were used as a contribution to purchase the system.

Table 7.3: Example of 50Wp system (Z$ prices end 1991, exchange rate US$1 = Z$5.72)

Components	Price	%	Life expectancy (years)
Panels	2550	45.5	10
Charge controller	200	3.6	5
Frame	200	3.6	10
Batteries 96Ah/12V	260	4.6	3
Cables and switches	200	3.6	5
Lights (4 × 8W) including fittings	560	10.0	5
Transport and installation (distance to dealer 200km)	300	5.3	
Dealer margin	850	15.2	
Sales tax (10%)	482	8.6	
Total initial cost	5602	100	

PV systems are to be compared with energy sources providing a similar end use. In rural areas the alternatives to PV are candles and paraffin wick lamps. The comparison with these sources shows that PV is cost effective when the discount rate is relatively low. This is normal because of the high cost of the initial investment.

5. ELECTRIC COOKING WITH MICRO-HYDRO POWER IN NEPAL

Nepal faces a number of challenges in meeting its energy needs. A landlocked country in the centre of Asia with no fossil fuel reserves of its own, it cannot afford to depend on expensive imported fuels. Partly because of this, and partly because much of the population lives in isolated mountainous districts, about 90 per cent of Nepal's energy consumption comes from biomass fuels.

The country is rich in one important resource: hydro power. Nepal has the potential to generate nearly 3000MW of power from its fast-flowing rivers in the Himalayas. The Government of Nepal has recognized this potential and the county's hydro power sector is developing rapidly. Medium and large-scale schemes are the main focus for providing power for the national grid. Only 10 per cent of Nepal's 19 million people have access to grid electricity. In view of the country's mainly mountainous terrain, extending the grid to reach these people will be slow and costly.

Decentralized, small-scale hydro schemes could make power available to around 50 per cent of the population. Mini-hydro and micro-hydro schemes are now beginning to emerge all around the county, providing power to villages that would not be connected to the national grid. There are now more than 800 micro-hydro

Ghandruk community electricity project

Photograph: Intermediate Technology/Steve Fisher

146

installations in Nepal. Most of these are used for agricultural processing, such as milling, hulling rice or crushing oilseeds, but more than 100 also generate electricity.

Using the example of Ghandruk, a mountain village in Nepal, this case study describes how micro-hydro power can help rural communities meet their needs. It also demonstrates how this power can be used for electric cooking, and the implications for saving fuelwood.

Bijuli deckchis in use
Photograph: Intermediate Technology/
Caroline Penn

Cooking with electricity

Lighting is an important priority for most villages, but electricity can also be used for cooking. Electricity has the potential to reduce the pressure on increasingly scarce fuelwood supplies. Since the existing electric cookers on the market are rated at least 1kW, they consume too much power to be viable in most micro-hydro power schemes. As a result, two types of electric cooker have been designed in Nepal, with rural communities in mind.

The *bijuli dekchi* consists of a cooking pot fitted with a low wattage element. It is used primarily to heat water, and also for cooking rice, lentils and vegetables. *Bijuli dekchis* come in a range of sizes (3 to 20 litres) and colours.

The *heat storage* cooker has an insulated block of stones for storing heat from a low-wattage electric element, which is on continuously. When cooking, a blast of hot air from the heat store is directed at the base of the cooking vessel. Because the hob can be used for frying foods as well as boiling water, the cooker may be a more appropriate choice in some districts, depending on local cooking practices.

Evidence is now accumulating to show that, in certain places and socio-economic conditions, electric cooking from micro-hydro can have a significant impact on people's lives and a beneficial impact on the environment. The case study of Ghandruk village illustrates this well.

The scheme and its location
The village of Ghandruk lies in the Annapurna region of Nepal, at the heart of the country's most popular tourist region. It is located on a steep hillside above

147

the Modi Khola river. The people are mainly farmers, though many households have a member who is a serving or retired Gurkha army member. Therefore, the village is relatively more wealthy than other Nepalese villages due to incomes from tourism and the army.

Pressure on forest resources has become an issue in the area since the pastoralist tradition of the area changed to more settled agriculture. Also, the growing local population and influx of tourists have increased demand on fuelwood.

The King Mahendra Trust for Nature Conservation started to address the resource problem in 1987, by looking into alternative ways of cooking and heating water, such as kerosene stoves and solar heaters. Solar water heaters were found to be too costly for most households and tourist lodges, though other alternatives were relatively successful. It was eventually decided to look into the potential for electric cooking with micro-hydro power.

The Ghandruk scheme generates electricity from a small stream, about a metre wide in the dry season. It generates about 50kW of power – enough to light the whole village plus a number of tourist lodges. In addition, 18 per cent of the households cook with electricity.

Most of the equipment needed for the micro-hydro plant was made by Nepalese manufacturers. It was installed by Development and Consulting Services, a Nepalese non-governmental organization which promotes micro-hydro power, with technical assistance from Intermediate Technology.

Economics

The 50kW scheme cost Rs.3 590 000 (US$72 000) to build, i.e, US$1440 per kW installed. Larger hydro power schemes in Nepal, for grid connection, cost two to three times more per kW than this.

Cooking with electricity
Photograph: Intermediate Technology/Lindel Caine

Ghandruk village provided 30 per cent of the cost of the scheme, half of which was given in the form of labour and half taken as a loan from the Agriculture Development Bank of Nepal. The remaining 70 per cent was provided in the form of grants and subsidies from the King Mahendra UK Trust for Conservation, the Canadian Co-operative Office, and His Majesty's Government of Nepal. A large grant was required to ensure that the project was

Information board at Ghandruk

Photograph: Intermediate Technology/
Janet Boston

sustainable and that the electricity would be cheap enough to encourage electric cooking.

Electricity tariffs were set at a level sufficient to pay back the loan within five years, and to cover maintenance costs and salaries (three local people were trained to run the scheme), while being affordable by all the families in the village. There were three different rates set, so that industrial and commercial consumers subsidized the rates for domestic consumers, with poorer families paying the lowest rate.

A village electrification committee was established with responsibility for overseeing all aspects of the project, from construction to tariff collection. Every family contributed labour to the project, which helped make the scheme viable and also gave a village-wide sense of ownership. Labour contributions included the carrying of materials, construction of the power house and civil works and installation of machinery and transmission lines. In return, each household was guaranteed electric lighting and the chance to subscribe to more power for cooking if they wanted to.

A fund was set up to provide subsidies for the *bijuli dekchis* to encourage people to buy them. The initial 33 per cent subsidy reduced the cost of the cooker to US$13 and US$20 for three- and eight-litre cookers respectively. A larger cooker of 20 litres, used by the tourist lodges, received no subsidy. In the first two years of the programme, 85 cookers were sold.

Impact on the community

Ghandruk's micro-hydro now supplies every household in the village with electric lighting. Only 18 per cent of the village can afford to subscribe to electricity for cooking, and the tourist lodges use about one-third of the total power. The higher tariff rate paid by the tourist lodges means that poorer families benefit from cheaper electricity.

Before the hydro scheme, families used between one and five litres of kerosene a month for lighting. To run one 25 watt bulb instead costs two-thirds of the price of one litre of kerosene. As well as being cheaper, the electric bulb provides a better quality of lighting. Other uses for the electricity include radio and TV, a grain mill and a small bakery.

Lessons learned
Lessons have been learned in the following ways:

- ○ Innovative approaches to matching rural energy needs with load development can result in a successful energy project.
- ○ This example shows where subsidies have been required to make the scheme viable. In this case it was decided that subsidies were suitable due to the environmental and social benefits of the scheme.
- ○ Local involvement in the project development was essential for the long-term success of the scheme.

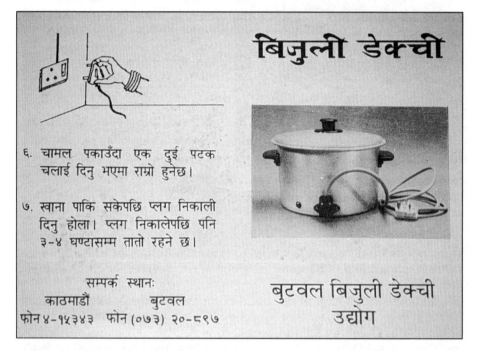

Instruction sheet for the dekchi

Photograph: Intermediate Technology

APPENDIX. GROUP EXERCISE: PV LANTERN DESIGN AND MARKETING

This book originated as a series of 'factsheets' developed by the Intermediate Technology Development Group to be used as a training resource for interactive workshops held in developing countries. In the course of running the workshops, IT's energy staff refined and expanded the factsheets to take account of the experiences and practical conditions of the participants, who came from many diverse countries of the developing world in Asia, Africa and Latin America.

The factsheets evolved into a 'resource pack' which, in turn, became this book. One of the valuable features of the workshops was a concluding exercise, which was designed to enable the participants to practice applying what they had learned to a 'real-life' situation. As well as testing the knowledge that they had acquired, the exercise required the participants to work in groups – thus fostering the element of productive co-operation that is essential when undertaking such an enterprise in the 'real world'.

This Appendix sets out the group exercise in exactly the form in which it was presented to the participants.

Introduction

This factsheet outlines a group exercise which will draw on the information provided throughout this resource pack.

The exercise is for three groups, which will examine:

Group 1. The needs of potential lantern users, their willingness to pay for the lantern and the features they want the lantern to offer.
Group 2. The technical specification of the lantern, including its casing, battery, etc.
Group 3. The process of commercialization of the lantern, including promotion, the supply chain from factory to home, etc.

Exercise background

This section gives you all the information you need to carry out the exercise.

Key players and their backgrounds
Raj, a 30-year old electronics technician, has taken over the family business in your region just two years after completing a design assignment with a European company specializing in photovoltaic (PV) products. Raj's father had built a medium-sized business manufacturing transistor radios and low-end music systems targeted at the large rural market of the region.

As this market was declining due to the availability of low-cost products from Hong Kong and Taiwan, Raj was contemplating diversification plans. Due to his

151

earlier experience in PV, Raj felt that a solar lantern for rural use could be a viable alternative as the factory had in-house capability in engineering, plastics and electronics.

Webank is a large donor agency with a mission to create sustainable markets for affordable technology among rural markets in developing countries. Webank's country representative, Peter was a development professional with experience in viable commercialization of affordable technology. In some of his earlier assignments in other countries he had success working with entrepreneurs in creating mid-sized appropriate technology markets for stoves and pedal pumps.

A plan was proposed and discussed

Raj first met with Peter at a party and they developed a rapport due to their common interest in technology. One evening when Peter visited the factory, Raj discussed his idea of diversifying into PV products. Raj mentioned that the entry barriers and cost of developing a sustainable rural PV market appeared to be so high that he was unable to risk this diversification. Peter was excited with Raj's plan and recognized that affordability was the most significant entry barrier. He pointed out that an earlier donor/government strategy of providing product subsidy to support affordability was actually anti-sustainability.

He felt that Webank could provide support in the PV product promotion by sharing responsibility and the entry risk in the product introduction process, by funding the initial expenses of research, promotion and supply chain setup.

Both agreed to start with a micro-solar lantern designed specifically to meet rural customer needs. Their brainstorming identified the following critical success factors:

- o full understanding of customer requirements from a lantern
- o product design and manufacturing processes that satisfy this requirement
- o a mechanism for delivery of the product to the customers and after-sales support

Raj assured Peter that he would develop a fully-fledged business proposal for creating a sustainable market for solar lanterns in the region. The proposal would then be used to secure development funds from Webank.

Key issues in PV production and marketing

After a lot of thought and discussions with his company staff and consultants, Raj felt that a viable project for the manufacture and marketing of the solar lanterns would comprise of the following three distinct segments.

1. Customer Evaluation: Accurate mapping of the potential customer profile, determining their lighting needs, ability to pay and desired product features.
2. Technology Evaluation: A technology scan to determine current products, design specifications, product configuration and matching technology to customer expectations. The key would be to arrive at a suitable product that was affordable to the target segment.

3. Business Plan: It is not enough to have a great product that the customer needs. The project will be successful only if the product is backed by a cohesive manufacturing/sourcing policy, distribution, promotion, after-sales and credit strategy. The business plan needs to integrate the above two issues and provide a viable plan for delivering the product to the end customer.

Raj decided to set up three task forces to examine each of the above issues and come up with preliminary recommendations. The group will split into those three task forces.

Task force assignments

Task Force 1

Assignment
Carry out an accurate mapping of the potential customer profile, determining their lighting needs, ability to pay and desired product features. The task force, based on its understanding of the rural areas of your region, should provide a complete customer profile for solar lanterns that can form the basis for selecting or designing a suitable product.
    In order to do this, you must consider the following key issues:

Key issues
  o The price that customers will be willing to pay for a solar lantern.
  o Definition of a suitable market segment for solar lanterns. The definition should detail:
    1. the income range of the target household
    2. probable location (such as villages, larger villages, district centres, etc.)
    3. education level and occupation profile
    4. other demographic or psychographic indicators that would help in identifying the potential market
  o Lighting needs assessment in terms of:
    1. number of hours lighting required per day
    2. reserve (stored) lighting capacity
    3. intensity of lighting required and colour of light preferred
    4. spread of lighting (i.e. full 360° or focused beam)
    5. preferred weight of lantern
  o Price–feature trade-off
  o After-sales support
  o Credit needs
  o Current lighting sources, usage patterns, level of dissatisfaction, etc.

Task Force 2

Assignment
Scan the different technological developments in the PV sector. Evaluate the different PV lantern options currently available and recommend a suitable

specification for the lantern. The specification should include the configuration of module, the design and colour of the casing, charge controller, lamp and battery.

In order to do this you should consider the key issues outlined in the following section.

Key issues
The common options that are available for consideration by the task force are briefly listed below.

PV module specification
There are two options currently available for the PV module.

o Thin film modules: These are the cheapest option. Thin film modules can be cut and configured locally to suit required voltage and power requirement. The module can be mounted on a simple frame. The disadvantages of this option include a fall-off in performance over time and lower efficiency in converting sunlight to electricity.
o Crystalline silicon: These modules are more expensive than thin film modules. The standard module size is smaller, and they are more efficient in converting sunlight into electricity. Technically, crystalline silicon panels are more difficult to encapsulate and assemble than thin film.

Casing specifications
You should consider the following options:

o Polystyrene: This can be shaped using high precision moulding but it is quite breakable.
o HDPE: This is a cheap material, but crude and a high quality finish is not possible.
o Polypropylene: Choose this material only if you are considering large production volumes. There may be problems with the availability of polypropylene granules.
o The lantern lens could be made of glass or polycarbonate. Each has its relative advantages and disadvantages.

Charge controller
The electronic user interface could be designed to cover all possibilities. However, the configuration of the circuitry needs to be evaluated in terms of affordability. The various options are low voltage cut off, over-charge protection, charge indicator and audio warning systems.

Lamp specifications
The selection of the lamp would be determined on the parameters of:

o wattage
o light colour
o life
o cost

- availability, and
- occurrence of tube blackening.

The options you can select from are:

- CFL
- white fluorescent lamps, and
- low-wattage halogen.

The selection of the lamp is interrelated to the battery and charge control configuration.

Battery specifications
Choose from the following options:

- Lead acid: This type of battery needs special adaptation for constant charging and discharging in the PV system. The battery is full of acid, so it is heavy, and as it is not sealed, can pose a safety risk. However, it is economical and easily sourced.
- Gel acid: Gel acid batteries are economical, completely sealed and commonly used in lantern application. However, they cannot be deep discharged and have a short lifetime.
- NiCd: Nickel cadmium batteries can tolerate deep discharge. They are very light and amenable to constant discharge and charge cycles. However, these batteries can be very expensive and suffer memory problem. Availability may also be a problem.
- Lithium iron: Technically, this type of battery is highly suitable for a PV lantern application. However, it is very expensive and not usually available in rural areas.

Task Force 3

Assignment
You must examine the commercialization process for the lantern.
Brainstorm the operational details of successfully transferring the lantern from the factory to the homes of the customers, and present the brainstorm in list or table format. Work out a tentative budget break-down for the promotion of the lantern and for creating a supply chain.

In order to do this you will have to consider the key issues listed in the following section.

Key issues

- Collaboration: Is there a need to seek partners who have specialized competency that would help in rural dissemination of the lanterns?
- Distribution logistics
  To work out the distribution logistics you should consider the following factors:

  - The distribution network (how many stages? what are the characteristics of the stages?)

- Trade margins (everyone takes a payment for being part of the network)
- Transportation problems expected (consider transport type, access to fuel, accessibility of target market)
- Role of local NGOs (can they provide information or training?)
- Trade training
- After-sales support (will the supply chain be sustainable?)

- Credit management: PV lanterns have a high initial cost, but no fuel cost. Credit management is a good way of spreading the high initial cost so that people find PV lanterns more affordable. This may need some support from the project. You should therefore consider some or all of the following factors:

  - Need for customer financing and amount of finance required, for each customer and in total
  - Can you work out if leasing of the lanterns is appropriate?
  - How would credit payments be collected? Will this impact on the cost of the lantern as a whole?
  - In reality, credit systems almost always contain some element of bad debt. Can you estimate the level of cover this project might need for bad debt?

- Promotion strategy
  In order to reach the market in rural areas, you need to consider the factors listed below. Use them to design the promotion strategy for the lantern.

  - Appropriate rural promotion tools (what will reach rural people in your region? Are there successful marketing campaigns in the past that you can learn from?)
  - Innovative promotion and demonstration ideas (consider drama and de-monstrations. What other techniques might work?)
  - Estimated promotion cost
  - Cost-sharing with supply chain (everyone involved in selling the lanterns will benefit from effective promotion – so others may be willing to bear some of the costs. People in the supply chain may also be closer to the customer than you are – so perhaps they may be willing to offer some time to talk to customers and demonstrate the lantern).
  - Manpower planning and structure (how many people will be involved in promotion? How will they be managed so that they achieve their aims?)

- Operational budget
  Outline the operational budget you will need to market the lantern. The budget should cover the following components:
  - promotion
  - bad debt cover
  - training costs
  - marketing manpower costs

References and Resources

Chapter 1

Foley, G. *Electricity for Rural People*, Panos Rural Electrification Programme, Panos Publications, London, 1989.

Hurst, C. and Barnett, A. *The Energy Dimension: A practical guide to energy in rural development programmes*, IT Publications, London, 1990.

Inversin, A. *New Designs for Rural Electrification: Private sector experiences in Nepal*, National Rural Electric Cooperatives Association, International Programs Division, USAID, 1995.

ITDG (Intermediate Technology) *Cook Electric: The Ghandruk experience*, Intermediate Technology, Rugby, 1994.

NRECA (National Rural Electric Cooperative Association) *International Program Report*, NRECA, Washington, 1994.

Smith, N. *Affordable Electricity Installation for Low-Income Households in Developing Countries*, Intermediate Technology Consultants, Rugby, 1996.

WEDC *Reaching the Unreached*, WEDC, Loughborough University and IT Publications, London, 1997.

World Bank *Rural Energy and Development: Improving energy supplies for two billion people*, World Bank, Washington, 1996.

Chapter 2

Gregory, J. et al. *Financing Renewable Energy Projects. A guide for development workers*, IT Publications, London, 1997.

Hankins, M. *Solar Rural Electrification in the Developing World: Four case studies*, Solar Electric Light Fund, Washington, 1993.

Khalizadeh-Shirazi and Shah, A. (eds.) *Tax Policy in Developing Countries*, World Bank, Washington, 1991.

OECD *Taxing Energy: Why and how*, OECD, Paris, 1993

Padmanbhan, K.P. *Rural Credit: Lessons for rural bankers and policy makers*, IT Publications, London, 1988.

Rodot, M. and Benallou, M. (eds.) *Energie solaire au service du développement rural*, IEPF, Quebec, 1993.

Seymour, A. and Mabro, R. *Energy Taxation and Economic Growth*, OPEC fund for international development (Pamphlet series) Vienna, 1994.

Wade, H. *Photovoltaic Rural Electrification Projects in the Pacific Region and Lessons Learnt*, South Pacific Institute for Renewable Energy, internal report, 1991.

World Bank/IFC (1994).

Chapter 3

Anton, D. *Diversity, Globalisation and the Ways of Nature*, IDRC, Ottway, 1994.

ExternE. *Externalities of Energy, Volume 1: Summary*, European Commission, Brussels, 1995.

Household Energy and Agenda 21 *HEDON, Discussion paper No.1, discussion paper of HEDON meeting*, Lund, September 28–30, 1995

MacDonald, M., Chadwick, M. and Aslanian, G. *The Environmental Management of Low-grade Fuels*, Earthscan, London, 1996.

Munasinghe, M. *Environmental Economics and Natural Resource Management in Developing Countries*, International Bank for Reconstruction and Development/World Bank, Washington, 1993.

ODA *Manual of Environmental Appraisal*, Overseas Development Administration, London, 1995.

WHO *Epidemiological, Social and Technical aspects of Indoor Air Pollution from Biofuels*, World Health Organisation, Geneva, 1992.

Chapter 4

Anon. *Diesel and Gas Turbine Catalogue: Engine Power Products Directory and Buyers Guide*, Diesel and Gas Turbine Publications, Wisconsin, USA.

Anon. *How Things Work*, Heron Books, London, 1963.

Anon. 'An investigation on the Colombian kerosene stove', *Boiling Point No.20*, December 1989.

Anon. 'Kerosene and gas stoves in Nagercoil, South India', *Boiling Point No.20*, December 1989.

Anon. 'Kerosene stoves in Ethiopia', *Boiling Point No.32*, January 1994.

Anon. 'Kerosene wick stoves', *Boiling Point No.20*, December 1989.

Anon. *The Power Guide: an international catalogue of small-scale energy equipment*, IT Publications, London, 1994.

Anon. *Rural Energy and Development*, The World Bank, Washington, 1996.

Desai, Ashok V. *Electricity*, Wiley Eastern Limited, New Delhi, 1990.

Fenn, J.B. *Engines, Energy and Entropy*, W.H. Freeman and Company, New York, 1962.

Floor, W., and van der Plas, R. *Kerosene Stoves: Their performance, use and constraints*, Joint UNDP/World Bank Energy Sector Management Assistance Program, Washington, October 1991.

Foley, G. *Electricity for Rural People*, Panos Publications, London, 1990.

Grauw, C. *Getting the most from your Diesel Engine*, Botswana Technology Centre, Gaborone, Botswana.

Hancock, D., Katerere, Y., and Moyo, S. *Rural Electrification in Zimbabwe*, Panos, London, 1988.

Louineau, J., Dicko, M., et al. *Rural Lighting*, IT Publications and The Stockholm Environment Institute, London, 1994.

Smith, Nigel. *Low-cost Electrification: Affordable electricity installation for low-income households in developing countries*, Intermediate Technology Consultants, Rugby, 1995.

Stone, R. *Introduction to Internal Combustion Engines*, Macmillan, London, 1992.

Walubengo, D., and Onyango, A. *Energy systems in Kenya: Focus on rural electrification*, Kengo Regional Wood Energy Programme for Africa, Nairobi, 1992.

Westhoff, B. and Germann, D. *Stove Images*, Commission of the European Communities

Chapter 5

Biomass

Anon. *Boiling Point*, Nos. 21, 26, 27, 28, 39, Rugby.

Gauser, M. *Power from the People: Innovation, users participation and forest energy programmes*, IT Publications, London, 1988.

Karekezi, S. and Ranja, T. *Renewable Energy Technologies in Africa*, AFREPEN, London, 1997.

Kristoferson L. A., and Bokalders V. *Renewable Energy Technologies: Their application in developing countries*, IT Publications, London, 1991.

158

Rosillo Calle, F. *The Charcoal Dilemma: Finding a sustainable solution for Brazilian industry*, IT Publications, London, 1996.

Stewart, B. et al. *Improved Wood, Waste and Charcoal Burning Stoves*, IT Publications, London, 1987.

Westhoff, B. and Germann, D. *Stove Images,* Brades and Aspel Verlag GmbH, 1995.

Biogases and liquid biofuels

Anon. *Biomass Energy: Key issues and priority needs, conference proceedings, 3rd–5th February 1997*, International Energy Agency, OECD 1997.

Gitonga, S. *Biogas Promotion in Kenya*, Intermediate Technology Kenya, Nairobi, 1997.

Gunnerson C.G. and Stuckey D.C. 'Anaerobic Digestion – Principles and Practices for Biogas Systems', *World Bank Technical Paper No. 49*, The World Bank, Washington, 1986.

Johansen, T.B. et al. *Renewable Energy Sources for Fuels and Electricity*, Island Press, Washington, 1993.

Karekezi, S. and Ranja, T. *Renewable Energy Technologies in Africa*, AFREPEN, 1997.

Kristoferson (1995).

Kristoferson, L.A. and Bokalders V. *Renewable Energy Technologies: Their application in developing countries*, IT Publications, London, 1991.

Ravindranath, N.H. and Hall, D.O. *Biomass, Energy and the Environment: A Developing Country Perspective form India*, Oxford University Press, Oxford, 1995.

Stassen, H.E., *Small-scale, Biomass Gasifiers for Heat and Power: A Global Review*, World Bank Technical Paper No. 296 Energy Series, World Bank, 1995.

Wind pumping

Fraenkel, P. et al. *Windpumps: A guide for development workers*, IT Publications, IT Power and the Stockholm Environment Institute, London, 1993.

Golding, E.W. *The Generation of Electricity by Wind Power*, E. & F. N. Spon, London, 1955.

Karekezi, S. and Ranja, T. *Renewable Energy Technologies in Africa*, AFREPREN/SEI, 1997.

Piggot, H. *Windpower Workshop*, Centre for Alternative Technology, Wales, 1997.

Smulders, P.T. and de Jongh, J. 'Wind Pumping: Status, prospects and barriers',Wales, *Renewable Energy*, Vol 5., Part 1, pp. 587–94, 1994.

Spera, D.A. *Wind Turbine Technology*, ASME Press, New York, 1994.

Wind power for electric generators

Anon. *The Power Guide*, IT Publications, London, 1994.

Golding, E.W. *The Generation of Electricity by Wind Power*, E. & F. N. Spon, London, 1955.

Karekezi, S. and Ranja, T. *Renewable Energy Technologies in Africa*, AFREPREN/SEI, London, 1997.

Kristoferson, L.A. and Bokalders, V. *Renewable Energy Technologies*, IT Publications, London, 1991.

Piggot, H. *Windpower Workshop*, Centre for Alternative Technology, Wales, 1997.

Spera, D.A. *Wind Turbine Technology*, ASME Press, New York, 1994.

Micro-hydro power

Low-cost Electrification: Affordable electricity installation for low-income households in developing countries, IT Consultants/ODA, 1995.

Rural Energy in Peru: Power for living, Intermediate Technology, 1996.

Fraenkel, P., Paish, O., Bokalders, V., Harvey, A. and Brown, A. *Micro-hydro power: A guide for development workers*, IT Publications, IT Power, Stockholm Environment Institute, London, 1991.

Hangzhou Regional Centre for Small Hydro Power *Small Hydro Power in China*, IT Publications, London, 1985.

159

Harvey, A. and Brown, A. *Micro-hydro Design Manual,* IT Publications, London, 1992.
Holland, R.E. *Micro-hydro Electric Power*, ITDG, Rugby, 1986.
Smith, N. *Motors as Generators for Micro-Hydro Power*, IT Publications, London, 1994.
Williams, A. *Pumps as Turbines: A user's guide*, IT Publications, London, 1995.

Solar photovoltaic energy
Derrick, A., et al. *Solar Photovoltaic Products: A guide for development workers*, IT Publications and IT Power, London, 1991.
Garg, H.P., Gouri, D., and Gupta, R. *Renewable Energy Technologies*, Indian Institute of Technology and the British High Commission, New Delhi, 1997.
Hulscher, W., and Fraenkel, P. *The Power Guide*, IT Publications, London, 1994.
Johansson, T.B. et al. *Renewable Energy Sources for Fuels and Electricity*, Island Press, Washington, 1993.
Karekezi, S. and Ranja, T. *Renewable Energy Technologies in Africa*, AFREPREN/SEI, 1997.
Louineau, J-P., et al. *Rural Lighting*, IT Publications and The Stockholm Environment Institute, London, 1994.
Twidell, J. and Weir, T. *Renewable Energy Resources*, E & F.N. Spon, London, 1990.

Solar thermal energy
Anon. *Boiling Point*, Issue Number 36, November 1995.
Garg, H.P., Gouri, D. and Gupta, R. *Renewable Energy Technologies*, Indian Institute of Technology and the British High Commission, New Delhi, 1997.
Hulscher, W., and Fraenkel, P. *The Power Guide,* IT Publications, London, 1994.
Karekezi, S. and Ranja, T. *Renewable Energy Technologies in Africa*, AFREPREN/SEI, 1997.
Twidell, J. and Weir, T. *Renewable Energy Resources*, E & F.N. Spon, 1990.

Case Study No. 4

Hawkins, M. *Solar rural electrification in the developing world: Four country case studies*, Solar Electric Light Fund, Washington, 1993.
Khennas, S. 'Strategies in the solar energy industry and South–North relationships', *Africa Environment*, Issues 20–22, 1985 (in French).
Ministry of Energy and Water Resources *Dissemination of Photovoltaic Systems in Zimbabwe*, Energy Programme Zimbabwe, Harare, February 1992.
Sudimara Marketing Strategy, Indonesia, 1995 (Company information).
Energy From the Sun: Photovoltaics, ITDG technical brief, Rugby, 1983.